Bullying: Replies, Rebuttals, Confessions, and Catharsis

D1416719

Bullying: Replies, Rebuttals, Confessions, and Catharsis

An Intergenerational and Multicultural Anthology

Magdalena Gómez
and
María Luisa Arroyo

Marisol —
you know the value
of preserving cultural
memory and that interrupts
a profound bullying that
is called erasure.
Gracias y Pa'lante,
Magdalena Gómez

Skyhorse Publishing

Copyright © 2012 by Magdalena Gómez and María Luisa Arroyo

Cover art: "Chantal" by Narelle Thomas
Cover Photo by: Kayla Creamer

All Rights Reserved. No part of this book may be reproduced in any manner without the express written consent of the publisher, except in the case of brief excerpts in critical reviews or articles. All inquiries should be addressed to Skyhorse Publishing, 307 West 36th Street, 11th Floor, New York, NY 10018.

Skyhorse Publishing books may be purchased in bulk at special discounts for sales promotion, corporate gifts, fund-raising, or educational purposes. Special editions can also be created to specifications. For details, contact the Special Sales Department, Skyhorse Publishing, 307 West 36th Street, 11th Floor, New York, NY 10018 or info@skyhorsepublishing.com.

Skyhorse® and Skyhorse Publishing® are registered trademarks of Skyhorse Publishing, Inc.®, a Delaware corporation.

www.skyhorsepublishing.com

10 9 8 7 6 5 4 3 2 1

Library of Congress Cataloging-in-Publication Data available on file.

ISBN: 978-1-61608-727-2

Printed in the United States of America

Dedication

We dedicate this book to Carl Joseph Walker-Hoover
and all who have died as the result of bullying;
to those who have died without acknowledgment or remembrance;
to all generations whose lives and self-esteem have been harmed due to bullying;
to those who remain beneath the fist of silence;
to all who have become bullies because they have been victims.

We remember and honor Jennifer Anne Fasulo
February 12, 1967–August 18th, 2010
for a lifetime of struggle against all forms of bullying and injustice.
Jennifer circulated her first petition at the age of 8 in protest of adult
bullying at her school. Jennifer lived a full and extraordinary life,
leaving a legacy of social change that continues to impact countless lives.
Never too young, never too late.

We honor Sirdeaner L. Walker
for her ongoing and dedicated struggle against bullying
on behalf of all children.

Contents

Schools

Acknowledgments

The Editors wish to thank all who contributed their writing to this anthology, making it one of a kind. We also thank all of the people and organizations, too numerous to mention here, who have supported our ongoing anti-bullying efforts.

Please visit: www.teatrovida.com for a more comprehensive list.

We thank Jennifer McCartney and Skyhorse Publishing for believing in this work.

Warm thanks to our Project Advisor: Iris Morales for her generosity of time, loving support and expertise.

Special thanks to: Jean Canosa Albano, Kayla Creamer, Fred Ho, and James Lescault for their support, and to Naomi Rosenblatt for her help in reviewing and editing the manuscript.

This project was supported in part by the Ford Foundation through a grant from the NALAC Fund for the Arts and AmherstMedia.org, Anne and Tom Eisenman, ALMMA (Association of Latinos at MassMutual and Allies), Baystate Health, Berkshire Bank, Community Foundation of Western Massachusetts, Hampden Bank, Hispanic Resources, Inc., Latino Breakfast Club, MassMutual Financial Group, NAI Plotkin & Associates, Springfield Housing Authority, Kim Parlengas (volunteer grants writer), and the Write Angle Writer's Conference.

Foreword

The impetus for creating this anthology was the suicide death of eleven year-old Carl Joseph Walker-Hoover, on April 6, 2009. After months of relentless bullying by male and female classmates at the New Leadership Charter School in Springfield, Massachusetts, Carl hung himself with an extension cord and was found by his mother, Sirdeaner L. Walker. The homophobic epithets that were part of the torment may as well have been bullets.

Ms. Walker helped bring national attention to her son's death and to the issue of bullying: "I just want to help some other child. I know there are other kids being picked on, and it's day in and day out." Ms. Walker continues to dedicate her life to bullying prevention and education. Bullying has always been with us, not only in schools, but also across all sectors of society.

This anthology captures a wide spectrum of stories in diverse genres, from people of all ages and walks of life. We are honored to feature well-known and new authors. We have created this volume out of a sense of urgency to provide venue for those who too often remain unheard, or whose stories are relegated to the sidelines as the work of "experts" takes precedence. Within these pages you will not find the words of the bullying "experts;" you will find the experiences of those who have lived it.

When I approached María Luisa Arroyo with the idea for this anthology, her response was positive, enthusiastic and immediate. The next day we put out the first call for submissions and were met with resistance and silence. Our attempts to get writing from local middle and high school students through their schools were the most discouraging. All of our continuous efforts, supported by several administrators, teachers, librarians, and which included newspaper coverage, radio and print ads, e-blasts, peer to peer outreach, social networks, flyers, and the offer to sponsor a system-wide writing competition with prize money, fell flat. We even delayed publication in the hope of getting submissions from the schools, but with few exceptions—all penned by adults—none arrived. This outstandingly low response underscores the failure of education that is primarily data-driven. The implied directive to "teach to the test" is exacerbated by the inherent pressures of living in our increasingly unimaginative, highly informed but humanly disconnected society.

The noble goal of nurturing critical thinkers has been replaced by rote, outdated ambitions to improve test scores. Everyone knows it, complaints abound, but we stay stuck, because as Dr. John Deasy, Superintendent of the Los Angeles Unified Schools put it: "Our schools are cash cows for researchers." When asked by an audience member at the Imag'nation Summit at Lincoln Center in 2011 if he worries about the "politics of his position," he responded: " I know what I know. I do it. I move forward. I keep my name on velcro on my office door." Narelle Thomas, a high school sophomore at the time she submitted work to this anthology at our personal invitation, spoke with us about her feelings on bullying: "Students are bored and angry. All teachers want is students to pass MCAS. We're not really learning; we're memorizing. If you have a question about something that is not on the test, they tell you not to worry about it. The school feels bad and everyone is tense. Students are really angry and the school feels more violent now. Those tests are bullying everybody." Narelle's words, and her image on the cover of this book, speak to the fragmentation of identity and the loss of self that come from being silenced—another form of bullying.

I recently visited a local high school where I witnessed the soul-numbing impact of classrooms that lack empathy. The teacher kept close proximity to his large desk, a vortex of contrived power. He lectured at the students, although we already know from the "learning pyramid" data that lecture only allows for 5% retention. We are aware of Howard Gardner's work on Multiple Intelligences, but it is not systemically applied. Who is training the trainers?

In this particular classroom I witnessed at least three students wearing ear buds attached to MP3 players, others with glazed-over eyes, yawning, racing their legs, frequently glancing at the clock, and otherwise appearing disengaged. A malaise hung over the room with the heaviness of a prison blanket. I became even more anxious than the students; I wanted to run out of the dingy room and into the sunlight. The students were passive, as if destined to remain unseen and unheard. The teacher was doing his job: conveying the curriculum material that would be on the standardized test. He did nothing to address the whole human beings sitting before him; he didn't see them, or simply ignored the nuances of submerged anger, frustration and defeat. He mimicked enthusiasm for his subject matter, but did not embody it. Young people are not fooled by the glitz of presentation; they need and want to feel the educator's passion and authenticity. I could hear the ticking of their hearts.

I have no doubt this young teacher started out his career with an altruistic optimism. However, by this point in his tenure, his energy felt caffeinated and appeared to come from a desire to impress his visitors in order to keep his job at a time when they are in short supply. Each student sat in his or her own protective bubble, detached from what should have been an enlivening, shared experience. Such detachment creates fertile ground for bullying. Once we cease to see and feel our shared humanity, to have empathy and connection, lively discourse and engagement, we become dehumanized. At the core of bullying and violence is the lack of empathy. It is this detachment from the sense that "we're all in this together" that allows for the objectification that creates bullies and their victims. If students are treated with a "one size fits all" approach to education, they begin to lose a sense of personal identity, individuality, and self-worth where their skills and unique intelligences are not recognized or applied. If individuals are not valued team players, or their contributions and gifts recognized, how will a cohesive team emerge? The resulting sense of alienation and voicelessness may lead a young person to simply become part of the inanimate "mob," a robot, frustrated, stressed, or simply very angry, as Narelle Thomas testifies, seeking out other ways to be seen, heard and respected. When we erase others or parts of them, we risk creating an emotional oligarchy of bullies and victims: those who disappear and those who disappear them.

The word "bully" often conjures male images, reinforced by mainstream media: cowboys, gangsters, greed-driven investment bankers, mean spirited school boys, killers, abusers, and the hyper-sexualized anti-hero, to name a few. Images that support the idea of superiority or domination of one group over another, or corporate advertising that strategically manipulates the passive viewer to feel defective or not-good-enough without their product, add to, or even incite competition, self-loathing and bigotry that can lead to violence.

In reality, we all know that bullies are male and female, come from all walks of life, are all ages, and everywhere: in schools, at home, in "nice" families, in the workplace, institutions, academia, corporations, media, the military, government, houses of worship, cyberspace, and the corporate advertising world.

The weapons wielded by bullies may be subtle and cumulative in nature, or immediate and extreme. It is the more subtle tactics that often go unnoticed, leading to the escalation of violence and victimization. Facial expressions, gestures, and body language can and do trigger violence—how many fights have started with "What are you looking at?" Capturing images of others for public use without their knowledge or consent can lead to cyber bullying and privacy violations, as in the noted case of Rutgers freshman, eighteen-year-old Tyler Clementi. Clementi was photographed during a private moment with another young man—and the image was posted over the Internet by his roommate. Tyler killed himself by jumping off the George Washington Bridge.

This is not an indictment solely of his roommate, who committed a heinous act of intrusion, but of a society where many LGBTQ youth must still live in fear, terror, or shame over their sexual orientation. A society that tolerates any form of bigotry and endorses it is complicit in the violation of human rights and crimes against humanity. Anti-bullying legislation will not stop bullying, until individuals as well as institutions, become *intentionally* pro-active in anti-bullying efforts. This includes what we model in our daily interactions. A simple thing, like throwing a candy wrapper on the sidewalk, shows a blatant disregard for others and disconnection from the world around us. Even the smallest actions speak volumes about consciousness and character.

I was raised in a South Bronx neighborhood where bullying was a normalized expectation, an inevitable part of growing up, defined as a "rite of passage." As a girl who stuttered, had a Puerto Rican accent and a lisp, was dressed in homemade party-like dresses, I had to learn self-defense at an early age. My father taught me to box, and my mother taught me how a knee to the groin would seal the deal with predatory boys. More than once, these skills kept me from being molested or even raped by older boys, for whom abusing girls was a badge of manhood, proof that they were not "faggots," and from self-loathing girls for whom I became "the freak" over whom they could triumph. After I broke a few noses, classmates began to attack me in groups. I remember being jumped on the way home from school by five girls armed with razor blades, who in the middle of winter, stripped me down to my cotton dress, taking my coat, school bag and the "emergency" money hidden in my sock.

Following that incident, my mother walked me to and from school until the eighth grade. I was tagged "mama's girl," and the attacks shifted to school bathrooms and corridors, where teachers looked the other way. Earlier in my schooling I was so afraid of going to the bathroom that I once wet myself, urine running down beige tights. I became "pee-pee girl," only to be trumped by "teacher's pet" as I was favored by most teachers for being intelligent, hard working, punctual, low maintenance, and always ready with correct answers. I aimed to please, not because I liked school, but because I knew that if I wasn't a diligent student, I would get a thorough beating when I got home by a mother and father who never had the chance to progress beyond the second grade.

Living in a culture of relentless violence and humiliation, I became the occasional bully, verbally tormenting and teasing those who were further outside of the margins than I was. I especially remember "buck-toothed, four-eyed" Mildred S. in her calico apron dresses and Buster Brown shoes. I began by hiding her books and coat, throwing her pencil case in the garbage, ridiculing her looks and disparaging her intelligence. I was only nine years old and never got caught. No adult suspected a "nice" girl.

I attended the Second Baptist Missionary Church every Sunday with my mother. It was there that I learned to unconditionally "Honor Thy Father and Mother," with teachers being their accepted proxies, regardless of their abuses. At home I learned that "what happens in this house, stays in this house," and mami was the equivalent to the Virgin Mary. Teachers embodied the Law and were to be obeyed under any and all circumstances. To question the authority of a parent or teacher was punishable by slapping, verbal abuse and beatings with a thick leather Garrison belt.

In keeping with the "sanctity" of motherhood passed down through generations, the basic rule in school was "don't talk about my mother." To have one's mother insulted and to not respond with a fist-fight made you the lowest of the low, a coward, a "faggot" and traitor to "all your generations," equal only to dog poop. A classmate, Carmen R., made the mistake of saying my mother was a "hua." I didn't even wait until school was out. I grabbed her in the hallway, and dragged her, by the hair, face down a flight of metal stairs. I saw her, flat out on the landing, immobilized with shock. I ran back to class, and the worst part of it all, I never got so much as a reprimand, because I was one of the "good kids." Until this day, it is the only regret I will carry to my grave.

My bullying phase came to sudden halt after that incident, as my conscience was more developed than my critical thinking. Eventually, Mildred and I became friends, when we both figured out there was strength in unity, and I realized that being a bully was neither pleasurable, nor wise. I had done it to be accepted by the "cool kids," who were more often than not, cowards, teasers, taunters and abusers who wore the hippest clothes, had the best looks, allowances, or simply oozed power according to our version of reality. I have no other memory of Carmen, other than her traumatized body at the foot of the metal stairs. Knowing I had defended my mother's "honor" did nothing to ease my shame and guilt. It took well into my forties to forgive myself, but I will never forget, and will be haunted with the question of what impact that act of violence may have had in Carmen's life and upon those children in whose life she may have played a part.

Just as one doesn't have to be a professional writer to tell the truth, one does not have to wait for permission to tell it. The sample below exemplifies the power of simple and direct communication, when young authors, in particular, are given venue to creatively share their experiences. The following poem is by Nakeishy Marie Fontán Sánchez, a sixth grader in the Holyoke Public Schools at the time she wrote this:

My sister Ruth

My sister Ruth
is 4 years old
she's diagnosed with
leukemia, but just because
she lost her hair or needs
to go to the hospital
every two weeks, that
doesn't mean she's changed
so stop it stop bullying her
cuz you don't know her

how I do even though
she's small, she has feelings
so stop and think would you
like it if you had
cancer and people laughed
in your face just because
you lost your hair or
have to get chemo-
therapy?

We have kept our editing to a minimum to maintain the authentic voices of the authors, regardless of their age or writing experience. You don't have to be perfect or a professional writer to tell the truth.

The cliché *"sticks and stones may break my bones, but words will never hurt me"* must be challenged. Words and looks can kill, and do. It was words and looks that killed Carl Joseph Walker-Hoover and countless other victims of bullying, most of whom do not make the headlines.

❖

"If you give information a story, you clothe it with a soul."
—Deepak Chopra

—Magdalena Gómez
Co-editor

Introduction

As I write this introduction, I cannot help but remember April, 2009 when I was still teaching GED classes at MCDI in Springfield, MA, the workplace I shared with Ms. Sirdeaner Walker, the director of the homeless program there. A few weeks earlier, I had run into her and her children, Carl among them, at the local Y and we talked briefly about private schools and our children's recent achievements.

On Monday, April 6, 2009, Carl Joseph Walker-Hoover hanged himself as a result of persistent bullying at his school, the New Leadership Charter School. I wouldn't learn about this until later in that week when Sirdeaner, a single mom, decided to speak with the press regarding the circumstances of Carl's death.

As a single mom, too, I could not imagine losing a child—let alone, in this horrific, incomprehensible way. At the same time, I felt compelled to act. I refused to hide my tears when I shared this news with my GED students, whose age ranged from sixteen to late fifties.

By then, the students had learned how passionate I was—and still am—about writing. Writing in one's own voice mattered. Writing in response to local, national, and international events—all of which impact our lives directly or indirectly—mattered. After allowing time for silence as we grappled individually with grief, the students and I dedicated classroom time over a period of days to write letters of condolences to Ms. Walker and to write letters to the principal of the New Leadership Charter School, which were copied to the superintendent of Springfield Public Schools. Regardless of their writing abilities, the students in their letters identified specific ways to address bullying in the schools. As promised, I typed up their letters and sent them to Ms. Walker, to the New Leadership Charter School, and to the superintendent.

At the same time, I shared my call to action with Ms. Magdalena Gómez, one of my closest friends, mentors, brilliant performance poet, and fierce artistic director and co-founder of Teatro V!da, the first Latin@ theater with a home base in Springfield, MA. She too decided to write and send a letter of action, one that reached even more people than ours did.

Moreover, Ms. Gómez encouraged all Teatro V!da ensemble members—especially the school-aged ones—to write and to submit responses.

Several weeks later, Ms. Walker, despite her insurmountable grief, acknowledged in person in my classroom the letters she received; letters, she said, that only underscored the importance of the unexpected journey she was now undertaking: advocacy against bullying. Ms. Walker added that, except for our letters and Ms. Gómez's correspondence, she did not receive any correspondence or calls from school officials, community leaders, or from the superintendent. To my understanding that day, Ms. Walker felt both devastated and fueled by this particular silence and felt—and stills feels—compelled to act by raising awareness about bullying so that other schoolchildren do not suffer what Carl did before he passed.

Outraged by the perpetuating silence in our community in light of Carl J. Walker-Hoover's death, Ms. Gómez put out a call for submissions for an anthology that addresses bullying . . .

In your hands, you now have this anthology. Why does this anthology about bullying matter? What makes this anthology unique or different?

This is our antidote for silence about bullying.

This is one way we can interrupt the silence of bystanders.

This is a *multicultural* anthology that carries the authentic voices of those who have authored their own experiences with bullying. These include students from middle school, high school, GED classes, and college; sons and daughters; teachers and administrators; parents and family members; nationally-acclaimed and emerging poets and writers; and everyday people.

Read this anthology—whether in order or randomly—and you will understand more profoundly both bullying and the routines of silence that exist in all the institutions that structure our lives: family, school, and workplace.

Read this anthology and you will discover that youth and young adults are able to name their own experiences with bullying and use writing as one of many vital tools they can use to dismantle the silence and to transform pain into resolution. At this point, I must state that the numerous submissions by Teatro V!da youth and young adults in this anthology contrast sharply with the absence of submissions from youth and young adults in the Greater Springfield school system, despite numerous and repeated calls for submissions. This suggests for me, as a poet, educator, parent, and co-editor of this anthology, that there is still so much work to be done in my hometown community and in our schools, in order to address bullying in a sustainable way and not treat it as a rite of passage or as a series of isolated incidents.

Read this anthology and be moved to act! Here are some of my own suggestions:

If you are a student:

1) Host an open mic night at your school, college, or local community center that ends with an open discussion about specific strategies to address bullying at school or elsewhere. Then act on those strategies.

2) Write and collect suggestions to send to your principal or director about ways that your school's culture can be improved. If your particular school is not receptive to the voices of young people, get your parents and adult family members involved.

3) Within your own peer groups, model and talk about respect of differences, and don't dismiss or ignore any little word or gesture of disrespect.

If you are a teacher:

1) Don't minimize bullying and do learn about your specific school's protocol to address bullying. If there is none, then advocate for one.

2) Incorporate one or more pieces of writing into your curriculum and create a classroom environment where students feel safe and comfortable enough to write and to talk about bullying.

3) Contact the editors of this anthology in order to find out how to invite them and/or any Teatro V!da youth members to visit your school for one or a series of bullying awareness workshops.

If you are a parent or a caring adult with a child or children in your life, I would like to share some strategies that I practice as a parent:

1) Foster communication at every age, even when the questions or situations each child or young person shares with you make you or your child uncomfortable, angry or sad.

2) Take appropriate action; this means: *bring a witness* to any meetings you arrange and put your concerns *in writing*. Don't leave voice mail messages; they can easily be erased.

3) If the adults in the school, the bus, or the space in which your child is are not responsive to your concerns, go above their heads *in writing* and send them a copy of your letter. In the meantime, make sure that your child is safe. If the situation becomes intolerable for your child, then make arrangements to transfer her or him to another space, and continue to advocate so that other children are not similarly impacted.

4) Whether or not the young person in your life has experienced bullying, pre-read on your own this anthology and identify sections or pieces of writing that you know would appeal to both of you. Then, as part of a family meeting or as part of your time with a young person, read aloud a section, a poem, or a testimonial and talk about it.

If you are reading this for your own understanding:

1) Don't hesitate to share your reactions with the co-editors of this anthology.

2) Volunteer to mentor a young person through any volunteer programs in your community.

3) Start a reading group with this anthology at your local library or community center.

As this anthology will attest, bullying is not a rite of passage.

—María Luisa Arroyo
Co-editor

INSTITUTIONS

"Violence is the last refuge of the incompetent."
—Isaac Asimov

Family

Unquestioned Traditions

Workplace

Internalized Institutions

Narelle Thomas
(written at age sixteen)

Why Schools Don't Work

School is not working as it should because in school there is no time to socialize; there are bad attitudes and negative feelings like stress, anger and discomfort. People are taking their lives because of these things. If schools are meant to prepare people while they are young in order to help them to learn and understand things better for when they get older, then the system should be updated as the times and people change.

The school schedule needs to change because many people aren't learning effectively because of it. There are about seven classes in a row for most schools. It's not healthy for people to be sitting for that long. Sitting constantly makes some people antsy and tense or lack energy. People don't usually get a chance to breathe unless it's time for lunch. At some schools the students don't even get to go outside in the nice weather. There should be a gym period and a period to go outside so that the students don't feel as trapped and have more breathing time to catch up with themselves. They would be more relaxed and open to learning.

Classes seem to last for so long and there are a lot of them. There should be less academic periods a day since people learn in different ways and do better when things aren't so concentrated into so many time slots. That would help with people's non-caring attitudes and improve the amount of people paying attention and doing homework. There should be physical and mental days where a lot of mental work is best done on mental days and physical on physical days.

There are right-brain and left-brain dominant thinkers, so it is better to accommodate both types to really make sure that "no child is left behind." There are two halves to a whole and without both there is corruption, because they are interdependent and neither is more important than the other. The right brain deals with the big picture, while the left brain deals more with a specific piece and separates things. Right-brained people need visuals more and use art-oriented things more. Left-brained people see the things that are in front of them, while right-brain thinkers see possibilities. Right-brain thinkers see more of how things work and process.

Left-brain thinkers see strategies and patterns more. Left-brained thinkers like their comfort zones and what they know, while right-brained thinkers tend to like risk-taking more. Activities that should be used are ones that activate and exercise both sides of the brain; things would work out better for everyone. Students should also be taught or shown in at least three different ways for people to understand. Since people learn in different ways students should also be able to listen to their MP3 players as long as it isn't too loud to disturb anyone and when they aren't doing group work or have to be listening to the teacher, because oftentimes people like listening to music for a stress reliever.

For students to be more attentive and interactive they have to eat well. Since people have so many allergies a suitable lunch or breakfast should have non-gmo (genetically modified organisms) food, more raw green vegetables, whole grains, fruits and beans and less meat, dairy, starches, sugars and salts. There should be foods that are good for people with diabetes and fruitarians and vegans too. Bad eating habits cause people to be hungrier and sleepier and so, their energy gets depleted because their foods don't have energy or many nutrients. If a more nutritious breakfast and lunch were served people would feel better, be less hungry throughout the day and there would be less people absent from school because of illnesses.

Certain subjects don't have the effects on students that they could. People usually learn things better when they feel that they can relate things to themselves or other things that they know or are learning about. The school history books aren't very inclusive of certain groups of people. It doesn't include much about Latinos to the point where some ask "is there anything about Latinos in the history book?" Many important events are missing in the books and aren't included in the curriculum. Africa shouldn't only be included for a week during Black History Month, and neither should Latino history only during Hispanic Heritage Month, to name a few. There should be inclusion in the curriculum throughout the year. Students feel their stories are left out of the history books so they don't connect history to themselves unless they associate it with something portrayed as bad. The people of African descent may feel victimized since one of the most emphasized things in the history books is usually slavery. Students really take things like that in and if people aren't explained things in detail and clarity they may begin to become ashamed of themselves and find things outside of themselves because they can't iden- tify with anything positive in a textbook. In English classes there should be more diverse literature besides Greek and Roman. Just because we live in America, it doesn't mean that writers from different places shouldn't be in our curriculum because America was built by people from many places and many people continuously come here. Students would learn to appreciate people from many cultures if they were exposed to them. Writ- ings are translated so there shouldn't be a problem. Youth should also be included in the books too, because students would also appreciate that and it would help them to see that if they work up to it then they could have their work expressed to help other people.

Leaving the classroom to go to the bathroom shouldn't be a strenuous process either; it should require a pass that the student and teacher both sign acknowledging that the student is going there and the time. Anoth- er option might be there being a bathroom pass for the females and one for the males and the person just tells the teacher they need to go to the bathroom, takes the pass and goes to the bathroom, because usually when someone has to use the bathroom they won't be able to fully concentrate until they do. The student would have a less boxed-in feeling because they know that they can take the pass and go. It would also help to increase the student's attentiveness because people don't like being denied use of the bathroom when they really need it.

Timed tests don't work well and neither do standardized tests because they tend to put pressure on the testers and hurt their grades because may- be they don't learn in that crammed kind of way. Studying for those kinds of tests are even hard for some people because often times many students find it hard and get nervous and tense, and tense learning environments don't promote learning or growth. Timed tests make many students rush to get their thoughts out and drain them for the whole day. A good alter- native might be to ask what students learned after each lesson and how it might be able to benefit them in another situation or if they create their own examples and work with them.

During vacation and after school, students should be able to rest a lit- tle because some students also have to work, help watch siblings, or might be involved in the arts, sports, after school programs, or volunteer work. Students involved in things like this don't enjoy coming home to seven homework assignments due the next day, especially if they're all the same kind. Teachers shouldn't send their students on overload with homework because of those activities and other homework assignments from other classes that are also due. There should be a variation of homework assignments, not just written. People learn in different ways, so the homework should include more than one way to do it. Vacations shouldn't be pounded with homework; they should respect vacation accommodations that might have been made. After a vacation without homework, students should return to school better rested and on point, since some students barely get sleep—which is detrimental to their potential and overall health.

Calling teachers by titles (Mr., Ms., Mrs., Miss., Dr . . .) doesn't always help student and teacher connections. Students may even rebel because of an imbalanced amount of respect that they feel they are getting. The student calls the teacher by a title and the teacher calls the student by their first names. The student feeling comfortable with the teacher can eliminate further respect problems. If the teacher has a problem with the students addressing them by their first name then they should explain it to their students. The students shouldn't feel that they are less than the teacher or as if the teachers' title gives the students less power. The student should feel equal to their teacher in that respect.

Teachers need to be relaxed so that the students can be relaxed with each other and can communicate effectively. There isn't time for students to socialize much because that's how classes are usually run. People need to talk more because that's how people learn more about each other and form bonds and learn to understand how people work. If more students were allowed to talk at some point during the class it would help them to solve things easier without always resorting to violence: socializing helps with good communication and developing those skills. A lack of good communication leads to fights breaking out and people constantly judging others because their communication skills aren't well developed. It makes sense to stop poor communication skills when people are still young so that as they get older their skills grow too and they are less likely to get into problems for it. Activities where students interact with each other, where they aren't forced into partners but have to pick someone new until they've worked with everyone at least once in the beginning would help them to be less stressed and have fewer negative feelings. They would learn more from one another while having a common goal to work towards together, which results in less bullying in classrooms and in schools in general.

There should also be good seating in schools like a good sitting surface for those who don't want to be at a table or a desk all of the time or when people need a little more space. There should be a round table where the teacher and the students could sit at together so that there isn't always a separation of everyone. Circles usually unite people and make them feel closer to each other.

Students work so hard in some classes only to get poor grades. Some take the time to do the work, but don't understand, struggle, stay after school and still struggle to pass. The grading system in schools should be one based on the honesty of the student, teacher and guardian. It shouldn't be based on what the student gets wrong and right as much as it should be on effort, participation, communication, and time management.

There should be an assessment at the beginning, middle and end of the school year that the parent, student and teacher are all a part of. The student should say what he or she expects of the teacher and the guardian(s), of himself or herself, and the work he or she will do to get to his or her goals. In the middle of the year, all students should write what they are doing to reach their goals and what they expect from themselves at that time. At the end of the year, they should state whether they got to their goals, did their guardian(s) and teacher meet their expectations, what they did or didn't like, what was most and least understood, and what they learned from the situation and class. In each instance, they should write down reasons why or why not. The teachers should complete one, stating what they'll do to get the students where they need to be and create a list of expectations for themselves, the students and guardian(s). In the middle and at the end of the year, the teachers should write self-assessments that students can read. Throughout the year, parent/guardian(s) should write assessments, too: what they expect of their child, of their child's teacher, and of themselves; what they will do to support their child; what they observed in their child; and whether or not the child and the teachers lived up to their expectations.

Teaching methods should not include victimization, accusing actions, or acceptance of unacceptable behavior. Teachers and students should both have the right to self-expression while holding themselves accountable for their own actions, respect for others and self, fairness and being aware of the consequences of their actions. School shouldn't feel like jail, especially for the amount of time that is spent there. It should be productive leading to fun, achievement and time well spent. When people think of school, they shouldn't sigh and groan; they should get positive thoughts and not a reminder of restriction and confinement. Slavery was implemented with fear and intimidation. Some teachers teach with intimidation and that makes people mentally unstable and isn't a good method to use. The use of intimidation to teach only shows that an individual is lazy and weak-minded or lacks creativity. Younger children sometimes pick up behavior from the adults around them; the action of intimidating people would be bad to pick up. Intimidation encourages low self-esteem and bullying.

If teachers had high expectations for all their students while helping them to reach their full potential, there would be no need to use intimidation. The use of encouragement or incentives would help the students and teachers alike to stay positive. This would help younger children especially because it would instill the fact that they can do anything that they work at. If a toddler is resistant to pick up a mess that they made in school, she or he would prefer and respond better to being told that his or her parent/guardian would be so proud. It won't work out so well, if the toddler is yelled at to pick it up or if they were told that their parent would be called. If the intimidation teaching method is stopped, then classrooms would be less stressful and more productive.

These are suggestions that I believe will help to highly improve the school system and make changes for the better. The only way to improve is to get creative feedback from the students as well as from the teachers and parents since we are all equally a part of the system. If a school system doesn't treat students, teachers, and parents as part of its whole, then it acts as a bully to the whole. Students and teachers should look forward to school as a place of betterment that is safe, that has friends and somewhere that they can learn. And if it is correctly done, it can be used as a springboard to propel them towards their goals.

Eilish Thompson

In Praise of the Media

They have written off the details
And condensed reality to fit the screen.
Their facts lie cold like concrete
(But we all know how the sturdy stuff shatters
And how the glass turns to shards.)

16,006 victims as of September the 5th 2009,
Six days before the fall,
Eight years ago,
And by now we should know every soul's name
By heart, and with heart
We should stand as straight as targets,
Adjacent to the rubble,
Parallel to the metal that was unbreakable and now
Bends at the middle as if praying for mercy
Like a child.

We should have news stories with names,
News flashes with names and not updates of cell phone upgrades,
We should have documentaries of every lost life—
What did he have for breakfast: did his wife cook him his favorite meal?
What did she wear, was it her mother's favorite necklace?
When they said goodbye to their children, did they know then?
When they stepped into history, did they know then?
Or was it only when the flames engulfed them
That they became conscious of their fate?
(But we know how hard it is to cope with reality. Or at least They do.)
We all should all be aware of the tears that bud and burst in any
    child's eye,
Or if there were ever smiles found on the survivors' faces again,
Or anyone who has felt the anguish of living
While others cease to live.
Their possibilities torment them.
All of them.

We all know the guilt that comes,
Like a price tag, with survival.

But I do not see that the actualities
In their careful diction match the intensity
That was written in blood like concrete in the faces
Made grotesque by the chemical explosion.
Nor do I see how they could.

For they have never drowned
In tempests of dust.
They do not possess scarred hearts
That are willing to broadcast truth
No matter the political cost.
And they have never experienced
The extremes of God's persisting promise of "free will,"
Only free press,
In which they are free to press issues
Of little importance
And slight catastrophes,
Denying names.

Marian Tombri

Temps

Temps that's what we're called
Little toy soldiers we are
Walking one by one, day by day into the danger zone
Battered and bruised
We still return for another round because that's the only place
    we have to go
Tiptoeing around
Making sure not to detonate
Not that easy with 10 pounds of fear, worry and stress weighing you down
Little toy soldiers we are, beckon to every call
Pick up the slack when one soldier's down
Pick up the slack when two
Pick up the slack when three soldiers down
Temps that's what we're called
We work too hard
And get little pay
But we always get the free sandwiches they give away
Shiny and polished new toy soldiers ready to take your place as soon as
    the next day
No matter how much time and effort you put in no one's ever safe
Permanents look at you with disgrace upon their face because their jobs
    are safe
Temps that's what we're called
Little toy soldiers that work too hard
Who get only one vacation day
Sitting around always wondering if today will be your last day
They will fire you with the turn of a cheek
All because they want to save money
Veterans of two years still get the ax
Slander your name
Beat you down
After you've done all they asked
Even kill you with a smile

All to hear those words your assignment has ended
I need it so I stay, but can get let go of any day
Temps is what we're called
Little toy soldier is who I will be
Until I get a permanent job offered to me

Nina Lydia Olff

American Gulfs: Knowing and Not Knowing

This is not a video;
the screech of supersonic bombs
is breaking ear-drums
and smashing skulls

This is a hell of white flames,
the gel is designed to cling to the flesh
until it burns down to the bone,
this is not

the rock-and-roll-apocalypse
of the Brando or Kubrick style helicopter,
the drone is redistributing waves
in sub-atomic particles.

The four-year-old alone with her dead parents is
trying to bring them back with kisses,
and she looks like my daughter—
Anne Frank in the eyes,

Is this Gaza?
Kandahar or Kabul?
Children walking to school must pass men excavating
bodies from under the piles of rubble,

Children are trying to walk to school
with instructions to avoid land-mines, Beware:
unexploded ordinance looks like juice-packs
from the first world.

Another Gulf of Tonkin collage of PTSD
False-flag to promote war—Distant War,
War that has become distant; fragments gone in the wind
like dandelions floating upward,

moving west from Babylon,
sun-dried dates heavy
with depleted uranium
apparitions of SAPS and the 'TonTon Macout.'

The slate has been washed and
our collective memory has been cleaned, we live
in a far off land where all is make-believe
and the bullies get carried away

just as green Ford Falcons
whisked away young mothers
pulled their arms out of their sockets,
dragged them out of their sleep in front of families;

to Be Disappeared
in downtown athletic clubs of Buenos Aires,
dropped over oceans with bellies slit
to make certain that they would sink.

America's Gulfs
are rivers uncrossed on broken roads
and the sorrow is popping out of the eyes
like crows;

even when we don't see the bodies;
or the women and men
who have been shouting ancient names
into the long night of centuries, while

watching their cities disappear like mist after rain,
their crops destroyed by locust armies, we sense
the breezes blowing from Auschwitz
and Rwanda will blow this way.

Estadio Nacional de Chile, the football stadium in Santiago, was once
turned into a giant open-air prison,
the sky-boxes were used for torture,
interrogations were carried out where all could witness

hundreds were executed between September 11
and November 7 of that year.
In locker rooms below
electric shock was administered to the genitals.

The space between
what is known
and what is not known
grows wider.

We have been put through the rinse cycle
of antonyms and repeat phrases,
designed to destroy memory and
your grandmother

as you are entertained
with the notion of celebrity.
Gangs of mercenaries from all corners of the earth
are multiplying like insects.

In Louisiana a football temple held the many.
The giant superdome was the coliseum of martial law—set up
to practice Homeland Security on Black dolls in the old south, who were
already hung and plucked.

The ghosts in that garden
will condemn us
for the sin
of just watching.

In Jackson Square
The statue of an Indian-Killer
who once fought along-side slaves
telegraphed the message of kings:

No More Congo Square,
No More Louis Armstrong Park
The death angel from the tomb of alligators and snakes
came to New Orleans and Baghdad.

The
water
is
rising.

Everything around you is corrugated
with untruth and illusion,
created
by a technologically-advanced platform.

Paperclips and other artifacts from WWII
are used to fashion parallel enabling laws
with Dr. Mengele as the role model
for atrocity to the other body.

I see your whole family
disappearing
like ice
in fire . . .

Crowd-control devices, first tested on Muslims and our prison
    population,
used on old people in wheelchairs and at Judge Rothenberg's School
    in Canton
Massachusetts; on "illegal aliens"
who came to earth from another planet:

(Colorado or California, Texas, New Mexico,
Teotichuatlan
and the land called Arizona . . . hey
my daughter and I look just like these strange beings . . .)

will be turned
on
all of
us.

These magic wands
have been perfected to deliver the shock of 50,000 electrical
volts. They were never designed to stun; they were made to
EXCRUCIATE.

I hope that you do not crack open
when the moon flies at you like a cannonball;
and squadrons of black operations
choosing chaos and entropy

move us further and further away from each other.
These special effects
will not be
televised.

Rick Kearns

Object Lesson/The Geometry of Rage

The hand that signs
the layoff list
the plant closing deal

is not the hand
that made the fist
in the apartment, last night.

The local thug
who hit him hard
when he was 13 or so

is not the rich man
trembling, standing over
the well-dressed but dead body.

The hands that hold
the biggest guns only
take, until there is
nothing.

Jennifer Anne Fasulo

From a Battered Women's Shelter
for the children

I. Tasha

You told me your secret
disguised as a story
so no one would get in trouble.
You told me the truth
behind the lie of your momma's smile,
but you told it aslant
for the danger, the danger.
Safe in my arms
between my whispered stories of magic
you told me your stories
that had no magic in them—
only brutality and naughty little girls
who get beat by Momma
for being bad.

I held you tighter,
but I didn't want to believe you
because your momma was my friend
and batterers were the enemy.

So I believed what I wanted to believe:
that you said Mommy
meaning Daddy,
that after watching him beat her
you imagined that she beat you,
that anything was true
other than the truth.

The other women were anxious
to comply with these lies.
They said, "She seems happy. It's the boys
we need to worry about. Have you seen
how they throw rocks at each other?"
I watched you
give your toys away
and play nicely on the make-believe
stove already cooking make-believe meals
for the make-believe husband. I listened
to your mother praise you
for practicing to be like her
and I said nothing.
I too, was relieved that your hand
was not raised in rage
against another child's skull.

II. Juan

The first time you ran out of the house
and into the street, I brought you back piggy-back
galloping to the sound of your laughter
tickling the back of my neck.
The second time that you ran out of the house
and into the street, I brought you back
somberly, your hand in mine, explaining
the dangers of fast cars and small children.
But the third time, Juan, that you ran out of that house
and into the street, I carried you back—kicking and
screaming, hating me then, as if I were all the people
who'd ever hurt and confused you for no good reason.
I locked you in the bedroom. I didn't know
what else to do. I told you I wasn't angry,
but I was—at the world for being so unsafe,
at you for being so helpless and scared,
and at myself for having to lock you up

to protect you. Good intentions never protected
anyone from a child's screams
and scream you did, such obscenities
I've never heard from a four-year-old child.
I left you there
because I had four other children
to take care of and only
two hands and
almost no more patience
on this one afternoon
that I glimpsed the predicament
my own mother faced
raising five children
day after day. And here I am
about to break
after three hours.

When I return to you
it is with an offering of grape juice—
your favorite kind. My shoulders
are braced against your fury,
but I find that even fury, that wretched companion,
has abandoned you to the empty room
where you lie in a heap on the floor.
When I come to gather you in my arms
you circle your hands around my neck and pull my head
close, your small lips almost touching my ear,
the question you ask is one that
nothing in my three years
of working here has prepared me to answer:
"Why does my Daddy hurt my Mommy?"

III. Jerome

My dearest Jerome
close those wide worried

eyes, so I might not see them
every night when I sleep, chased
by the immensity of your need
and the needs of the thousands of
children whose eyes I do not see.
It's been months since your
momma stole you away in the middle
of the night without a word
to anyone, back to Pappy
and the horrors of home.
Someone heard her say, "I'd rather
be smacked than spend another night
in this place." You go with the clothes
and the lipstick and the make-shift suitcase,
you go because Momma goes,
you don't choose, you go.
Never knowing why I didn't come
to take you roller skating, why promises
shatter like glass against the pavement,
why all adults smile
and tell lies.

I wonder when I wake
from troubled sleep where you
are and whether you think of me.
I wonder whether we will ever meet
again when you are grown, if you'll
remember the way we loved, as if we
knew each other a lifetime instead of
three short months.
Or would we meet instead
enclosed in our separate worlds:
Man and Woman
Black and white,
Unable to see one another or
touch the indiscriminate loves
that children leave behind.

Will you know the reason I
could not come for you?
When you grow to be a man, will
you turn to strike a woman like
your father taught you?
If she comes to me in need,
will I dismiss you as the enemy
forgetting how we once loved
how I was forced to abandon you
to the killing streets and the
war-torn walls of your own home
where you sat with your great grief
waiting for someone to come.

Janice Levy

Even Diana Ross Has Backups

Turning 13; reciting prayers in the Rabbi's office. My father squirting nose spray, my mother dabbing her stocking runs with clear nail polish. Eating pastrami sandwiches at the Carnegie Deli, the waiters toasting us with Dr. Brown's Cel-Ray Soda.

A week later, Layce Cornish celebrates her Bat Mitzvah in a catering hall with chandeliers and butlers. She has a sitting- on- her- right- side best friend, a left- side best friend, a best camp friend, a best homeroom friend, a best cheerleading friend, a best in- each- of- her- classes friend. I'm assigned to the "neighborhood table" with the boy wearing mailman pants, Spanish Maria and a kid from Romania known as "The Bat."

My parents drop me off and gawk; my mother still wearing her bowling shoes, my father smelling of peat moss.

Mr. Cornish wears a tuxedo and shit-kicker boots. His hair is violently slicked back.

A Jewish cowboy, my father whispers. I never heard such a thing.

My mother draws a finger across her throat. The people he knows—you could end up like lox.

Mrs. Cornish wears big sunglasses and a scarf. Who does she think she is, my mother says, fucking Jackie Kennedy?

After dinner, we watch "That Darn Cat;" Mr. Cornish running the movie projector, waiters passing out popcorn. A horn blasts thirteen times, then once more for good luck and we run outside to see Haley Mills jump out of a limo, carrying a cross-eyed Siamese cat named "D.C." with a wristwatch around its neck.

Layce! Lay-ceee!

The room spins like a tornado.

After the party, all the girls sleep at her house.

Guess who's growing a mustache, she announces, studying me, picking Cheese Doodles from her teeth. She calls me "Flatty Patty" and says I have an anteater's nose. I fake a migraine and call home. My fathers' cranky, his robe furious; I've made him miss the June Taylor Dancers on the Jackie Gleason Show.

Man my age, he says, any woman spreads her legs I watch.

My mother, smelling of Noxzema, spit curls taped to her cheeks. Who died? Her voice shoves. Get back out there and play the field.

What are you talking, my father says. This one, she couldn't catch a cold.

In ninth grade, I'm chosen class valedictorian. My father, a sign maker for Sears, writes my speech. My mother is my vocal coach. Around, she makes me repeat, poking my cheeks. Town, frown, brown. A dress is bought; too this, too that, but you're not Cinderella it's just a graduation speech, junior high no less. I am reminded to sit up straight so I don't look like a hunchback.

Before the ceremony, I watch the principal shake Mr. Cornish's hand, thank him for the first row circus tickets. His grandson riding an elephant in the center ring, dancing with the clowns, the excitement, don't ask.

At graduation, Layce gets a new award, a special award; nobody's sure what's written on the plaque. She throws her hat in the air, prances like Jim Morrison: break on through to the other side! The room erupts.

When I'm introduced, a sneeze spreads from row to row. My mother mouths my speech, my father keeps turning his head around, as if he has lost someone but forgotten whom.

Someone barks. I drop my index cards, hit my head on the podium.

A single voice. A signal.

Cough, cough, cough.

An outside door opens. Wind blows up my dress. A camera flashes.

Whoosh! My father cackles afterwards. Like a regular Marilyn Monroe.

My mother mutters something about a car accident, clean underwear, and Dear Abby.

I count-count-count the names on my Sweet Sixteen list. My carpet is a war zone; seating charts detonate, place-cards charge like tanks. I cross-out, star, and highlight. I send out invitations eight weeks in advance.

My eye twitches. A rash of thorns grows on my chin. I cough up exhaust smoke. For days I eat only lettuce and laxatives.

I wait for the mail. Count-count-count.

I get an inhaler, reading glasses; there is something with my gall bladder. I pick at a sore behind my ear.

Who shall live and who shall die, my father intones.

The caterer says the room will look fuller with balloons. The folk singer comes down with lung cancer.

One less, my mother says.

Count-count-count.

Suddenly, Layce switches her party date. Everyone on my list is on hers plus a zillion more.

My mother invites her hairdresser, dry cleaner and second cousins from St. Louis; they've always wanted to see the Statue of Liberty, she says. Even Diana Ross has backups.

Then this:

Spanish Maria is expelled from school and rips apart her locker. I grab an unused notebook, a gray scarf and a handful of firecrackers stuffed in a soccer cleat.

That night while my parents watch The Flip Wilson Show in their bedroom, I slip out, get my bicycle from the shed.

Layce's porch is still strung with paper lanterns and flabby Happy Birthday balloons. I lay my bike down, hide behind a tree. I hear the television blaring; Geraldine is smart-assing her boyfriend, Killer.

Feeling in my pocket: Black Bat, Black Cat, Atomic Flashlight Crackers. The cover of The Cherry Bombs shows three fruits on a branch.

Reading the directions under an open window: Lay on ground, light fuse, and get away.

Striking a match.

Geraldine sassing, What you see is what you get.

I pedal home, feeling parts of me breaking off in the wind. Lying in the dark, arms gripping the sides of my bed, breathing double-time; as if eaten by the sea.

You hear the sirens?

My mother complains in the morning. After Flip did the Reverend LeRoy bit. My father says the ambulance made our house shake.

The Cornish house is sold in four days. Neighbors say there was blood all over the place.

·············

Thirty years later, the bathroom lights at JFK Airport go out.

Screams, bodies tripping in the darkness. I hide under a sink.

Cell phones switch on, lighters flick. Someone sprays a flashlight in my face.

"Hey, you know me, don't you?"

I shrug, blinking as if I have a tic.

"I'm Layce Cornish. Didn't we like car pool in high school or something?"

The lights stutter. A police officer shouts into a megaphone, herds us outside.

Layce reciting in my ear: There's the labradoodle she cloned for $50,000, the yearly China trip, her 40th Surprise Birthday Party catered by Rachel Ray.

Feeling up her knapsack for photographs, looking me over as if squeezing cantaloupes.

"So what do you do and who do you know," her voice ticket-tapes. "I forgot your name. Spanish Maria, right? Your madre cleaned our casa."

Something settles hotly in my cheeks. I smile with my lips.

"No husband? No children? Ommigod!" Her lower lip juts like a window sill.

"You move away," I say.

"Doesn't everyone?"

Her laughter spiking the air.

Mine dribbling into a tissue.

Layce waves to a man carved from a cedar tree, a man who can wear all white and not look like he sells ice cream. A man with rumba in his hips, an accent on his lips, smiling as if my blouse has slipped off.

Layce grabs his shirt collar, chews up his mouth.

We are not introduced.

If I'm ever in L.A., Palm Beach, Southampton, I'm to look her up, she says, her cheek against mine, and I see that she's airbrushed; her face a tight canvas, her teeth a shade lighter than the moon. Also this: her right nostril is bigger than her left; underneath, two little scars swim like fish.

Over the PA system a voice repeats: There is a courtesy call for a Reverend Le-Roy Wilson. Reverend Le-Roy Wilson, a courtesy call, please pick up.

"Who did your nose?" I ask.

Her gaze snaps.

She goes for a smile, then stops.

Eilianie M. Alvelo

Pregúntale a las luciérnagas

Aquella vieja casa de madera con techo de zinc lo sabe. Las luciérnagas alumbraron un poco la oscuridad de esa noche; y de esa noche fueron testigos. Afuera llovía y las gotas conversando con el zinc junto a la Corrientes del Río la Plata, y el canto del coquí, fueron mi canción de cuna. Yo dormía y no era la primera vez que la misma melodía me acompañaba en el mismo lugar. No recuerdo cuanto tiempo tuve para soñar; y me pregunto ¿por qué mis sueños fueron interrumpidos? ¿Cuándo pasó por su mente por primera vez? ¿Fue espontáneo? ¿Por qué a mí? . . . Llevo doce años con tantas preguntas nacidas de aquella noche. Tenía seis cuando dormía y sentí sus manos tocándome en . . . en esas partes de mi cuerpo. Yo no sabía lo que él estaba haciendo, pero estaba segura de que eso no era correcto. Mami me lo había dicho: "Nena, no te dejes tocar tus partecitas." En el momento en que desperté él ya estaba con su cabeza . . . Pues ahí. Cuando él estaba haciéndolo me preguntó que si me gustaba. No respondí. Lloraba. Le comencé a patear la espalda mientras él lograba callarme. Él seguía y seguía, y yo tratando de que ellos, de que ella me escuchara y en el intento, logré que se alejara de mi cuerpecito. Asustada no dormí. Siempre detrás de aquella puerta antes de ducharme, lloraba cuando miraba mis partes. Pasaron dos años y aterrada en el eco de su amenaza de hacerles daño, ávidamente callé. Hasta que esa puerta se abrió y en el lloriqueo fui forzada a decir que él me robó la niña. Mami abrazándome desconsolada y como si yo no la entendiera decía: "¿Por qué? ¿Por qué le tuvo que pasar a ella, a mi bebe, lo mismo que me pasó a mí? . . . ¿Qué dices, mami?," dije y ella solo contestó: "La melodía de la lluvia tropezándose con el zinc, el 'coquí, coquí' por todas partes y las luciérnagas irradiando la oscura noche nos llevaron a dulcemente a soñar . . . hasta que él llego. Yo sé, las luciérnagas lo saben." . . .

Eilianie M. Alvelo

Ask the Fireflies
(translated by María Luisa Arroyo)

That old house of wood with the zinc roof knows. The fireflies illuminated a little the darkness of that night and, of that night, they are witnesses. Outside, it rained and the raindrops which talked to the zinc roof, the currents of the Río de Plata, and the song of the *coquí* were my lullabies. I would sleep and it wasn't the first time that the same melody accompanied me in the same place. I don't remember how much time I had to dream and I asked myself, "Why were my dreams interrupted? When did that occur to him for the first time? Was it spontaneous? Why did it happen to me?" . . . For twelve years, I have been carrying so many questions born of that night. I didn't know what he was doing, but I was sure that it wasn't right. Mami had told me, "Girl, don't let anyone touch your little parts." In the moment I awoke he was already with his head . . . well, down there. When he was doing it he asked me whether I liked it. I didn't respond. I was crying. I began to kick his back while he succeeded in keeping me quiet. He went on and on, and I was trying to get them, to get her to listen and in the attempt, I managed to get him off my little body. Terrified, I didn't sleep. Always behind that door before taking a shower, I would cry while I looked at my parts. Two years passed and, terrorized by the echo of his threat to harm them, I remained avidly silent. Until that door opened; while sobbing I was compelled to say that he robbed me of my childhood. Hugging me inconsolably and as if I could not understand her, Mami said, "Why? Why did it happen to her, to my baby, the same thing that happened to me?" "What are you saying, mami?" I asked and she only responded, "The melody of the rain crashing into the zinc roof, the coquí, coquí everywhere, and the fireflies illuminating the dark night brought us sweetly to dream . . . until he came. I know, the fireflies know." . . .

Emmy Cepeda

El tiempo de las muñecas

Con mi muñeca, jugando en el balcón
Un, dos, tres bailábamos los dos
Nadie en la casa, él susurró
Un, dos, tres así me abrazó

Jugando, alegrías cultivó
Poco a poco mi confianza se ganó
La muñeca miraba
Pero en sus ojos la luz no brilló

La hora de jugar ya terminó, en un cuarto oscuro él me llevó . . .
Un, dos, tres la luz se apagó
¿Por qué estoy sintiendo la crueldad de tu olor?
Un, dos, tres ya todo cambió

Aquellos ojos deseosos y esa voz diciendo que nó
No te lleves mi vida, no te olvides quien soy
Recuerda la niña que una vez te adoró

En mi piel penetras tu enfermedad, penetras tu obsesión . . .
En un, dos, tres la inocencia borró
Mi vida en dolor se convirtió
Un, dos, tres solo la muñeca vió lo que pasó.

Emmy Cepeda

In the Time of the Dolls
(translated by María Luisa Arroyo)

With my doll, playing on the balcony
One, two, three, we used to dance, we two
No one at home, he murmured softly
One, two, three, that is how he hugged me

While we played, he made the joys grow
Little by little, he gained my trust
The doll used to watch
But in her eyes the light did not shine

When the playtime hour ended, he brought me to a dark room . . .
One, two, three, the light went out
Why am I feeling the cruelty of your smell?
One, two, three, now everything has changed.

Those eyes that pleaded, that voice that said, No
Don't take my life. Don't forget who I am
Remember the little girl who once adored you.

Your sickness penetrates my skin as does your obsession
In one, two three, innocence was erased
My life has been changed to one of pain
One, two three, only the doll saw what occurred.

Carolyn Durán

Miedo al ayer

Ayer te ví otra vez
rondando en mis sueños
aquel que me arrancó la inocencia con sus manos.

Ya no río más, ahora cubro mi ser con algo que no soy.
Tratando de escapar de esta telaraña que hicieron tus recuerdos.

Sentir que por un tiempo te vas,
pero no sirve de nada
tu recuerdo se aferra más a mí.

Perdí aquella niña inocente que
sonreía cada vez que te veía.

¡En las noches ya no duermo tranquila!

Todavía puedo sentir aquella respiración
me repugna el recordarte
me asquea el poder sentir tus manos recorriendo mis piernas.

Tratando cada día con olvidarme de tí,
de aquella tarde llena de miedos y
lágrimas recorriendo mis mejillas.

Y aunque todavía me da terror escuchar tu nombre
algo no me deja odiarte

apesar de todo TE QUIERO!

Usted, señor de edad,
aquel con el que jugaba
al que le llamo tío!
gracias a usted desconfío
ya no soy más risueña!

Aquella tarde se fue contigo mi tranquilidad . . .
Ya no duermo más!!

Carolyn Durán

Fear of Yesterday
(translation by María Luisa Arroyo)

Yesterday I saw you again
making the rounds in my dreams
you who tore from me with your hands my innocence.

I no longer know how to laugh, now I cover myself with something that I
    am not.
Trying to escape that web that memories of you have made.

To feel that you will leave for a while,
but it doesn't matter
the memory of you clings more to me.

I lost that innocent girl who
would smile every time she saw you.

Nights, I have stopped sleeping in peace!

I still can feel your breath
remembering you repulses me
the sensation of your hands running up my legs disgusts me.

Trying every day to forget you,
that day full of fear and
tears dripping down my cheeks.

And even though it terrifies me to hear your name
something in me doesn't let me hate you.

In spite of everything I LOVE YOU!

You, older man,
the one with whom I played,
whom I called *tío*!
Thanks to you, I no longer trust
I am no longer the smiling one!

That night my peace of mind left with you . . .
And I can no longer sleep!

Robin Coolbeth

Will You Know Me In Heaven?

When you get to heaven and pass through those pearly gates, will you have put your grievances and biases behind you? I should think they wouldn't matter in the happiest of places. But I am not as religious as you so I could be mistaken.

You told me that you're guaranteed a seat up on Cloud 9. Your pious acts are well publicized. You sing the loudest in church, leading us in hymns.

I don't know all the words and the harmonies sound flat. But I will trust your expertise on scripture and all that.

You're correct; I do not follow all the teachings of the church. I try to live by the Golden Rule and the "do unto others" thing. When you visited last week, you told me that that is not enough. I must completely follow all the teachings of the clergy; otherwise I will be left in the dust. But what if you are mistaken and St. Paul does let me in to join the fun.

Will you know me in heaven?

When I get my wings, I will say hello to you.

I will say hello to everyone—even the Jews.

I will say hello to the Homosexuals and the Buddhists too.

If goodness at heart is enough, we will be the faithful flock.

Will you think you are in the wrong place or that a mistake has been made? When I smile at you, will you smile back?

Or will you be put off at seeing such a riffraff crowd?

Will you know me in heaven?

I can see I've gone too far now. You are frowning and quite upset. The minister said asking too many questions would get me in trouble and here I go again. Forget about what I have said. I could be totally wrong, and perhaps I am doomed. We will agree to disagree.

After all, faith is a powerful thing.

Sandra María Esteves

Too Beautiful For Words

for Nicole

Below is a poem I wrote in 1995 when the TV news announced that OJ Simpson had been acquitted for the murder of his wife Nicole. The poem talks about the concepts of ownership and domestic violence within personal relationships and the disastrous consequences that result.

In the peak of her life
he had to possess her
wanted to own her
She resisted control

She was just
too necessary a treasure
not to belong to him

He needed to have her
Had to own her
the way he owned designer socks
that embellished his feet
Owned the wide-body mini-van
power symbol of his manhood
Proof of his ability
to control
His driving need for ownership
Insisting she comply
conform to standards of possession
Fit into formulations of acquisition
Offering evidence
he had it all
owned everything
could show the world
the measure of the man he was

Without question she belonged to him
Bought and paid for
like the deed to his house
like the jeweled watch and fancy glove wear
he owned
like the shined shoes and tailored European suits
he owned
like the extensive selection of silk ties
all declaring "He owns us!"

She was just too gorgeous a specimen
too fine a thoroughbred for him not to own

Especially when she insisted
I belong to no one! I belong to myself!

Especially when she resisted
though bought and paid for
like some market slave

She had to be punished for her sins
Had to pay for every insistence
against ownership of her spirit
She had to pay for her resistance
He had to make her pay
to prove his power
his claim to possession
his nine-tenths of the law
that owned all of her
—the whole of her

No discussion or arbitration
no negotiation
Just unconditionally his
Each strand of her feminine head
each pore of her well-pampered skin

each corpuscle of pulsing cells belonged to him
Not only the diamond ring and gold band
he owned the finger as well
the hand it was on
the muscles and tendons that moved it

How dare she deny his right to possess
against her right to resist
His need to control
against her need to self-determine
the path she would follow

She was much too exquisite
a flawless facet
an asset to the package that defined him
according to his definitions

She had to pay for her sins

He had to prove he owned every part
Her words. Her thoughts
She could not—should not think for herself

He owned her mind
Her time was all his
Whenever he demanded—needed
to stroke his ego again
to remind himself
he was still—and always
a man who owned

She was not worthy to command herself
Did not deserve to be master of her being
She belonged to him
like his bank accounts belonged
his c.d.s and i.r.a.s belonged
his state-of-the-art entertainment technology belonged

his media channels and running trophies belonged
claiming and proclaiming he was the fastest and the best

He owned her totally
the way some women are owned by men who claim them
who own every bone that breaks
every tuft of hair that is yanked
every bruise and cut
every anxious churning and wrenching

He owned her, body and soul
He owned her mouth and her tongue
her breasts and her clit
her vagina and her womb
he owned her sex and her hormones
her monthly juices and physical functions

Like the clothes she wore
he also owned
her orgasms and fantasies
her swollen belly and her children
Every breath was his
every inhaling and exhaling
every moving of her diaphragm
every heart pulse and rush of blood

He owned her voice
every prayer she invoked
every tear that surfaced
was his to taste and savor
to absorb and to consume
to digest
to throw away
and discard—at will

. . . to eliminate . . .

However it pleased him
whenever it moved him

She was not supposed to
resist
Possessions are not supposed to
talk back
or fight for their autonomy
Not supposed to return an insult
or throw back a punch
in self-defense
or pick up a gun

Things that are owned have no rights
other than being owned
other than belonging to their owners
obediently—and silently
No rights that fit into his rule book
of acceptable plays
that don't conform
that step out of boundaries and cross lines
that would be laughed at by the fellas
criticized by his peers
No place for original thinking
or innovative ideas

No space for sharing or dialogue
No room for equality or discovery

(Like being scared of your own shadow
or afraid to feel your own warmth.)

It wasn't enough to bask in her light
He had to possess it too
as if he had no light of his own
As if possessing hers
automatically guaranteed his

As if he never learned to find his light
or cultivate the greater possibilities
within himself

She had to pay for her sins

She paid
every time she spoke out expressing an opinion
She paid for all women who ever spoke out and disagreed
She paid cumulatively
for every challenge that ever confronted him
For his inability to love himself
and accept his ordinary human qualities
She paid for his unfaithfulness
(Of course, that was her fault too)
She paid for all the terrible things he did
Because . . . she made him do it
Even though she never twisted his arm
or inflicted a black eye
It was clear she cast a spell over him
which was the root and cause of his miserable life
She paid for his loudness and lustfulness
his restless impatience and loneliness
his ambivalence and indifference
She paid for every unfulfilled desire that ever frustrated him
Every unreachable ambition that overstepped his potential
Every bad dream and negative omen
She paid for his misplaced things and mistrust
His confusion and drug use
She paid for the abuse he gave
and for the abuse she received
She paid for his extensive lack of respect for all that he was
His lack of respect for all that she was
His blindness in appreciating her worth
His incomprehension of the wholeness of her being
She paid for her refusal to indulge his faults
or wallow in his mud

He owned the inner being and essence of her
—lock, stock and . . . barrel

She had to pay for each day and night of suffering
he endured in having to live with himself
for the color of his skin and the hostile environment that hated him
that held him back for being all that he was
that did not allow him to struggle or strive for holistic values
or find peace within being himself

She had to pay for everything

She belonged to him
She refused to be owned
She had to be punished for her sins
She had to pay

. . . with her life . . .

And not only that—
Her friends paid with their sorrow
Her family paid with their grief
And her children are still paying
and will be paying for a long time to come

And every other person who will ever become a victim is going to pay
Maybe even some of you sitting in this room
hearing or reading these words
unless you get up and leave
unless you rescue yourself

Every six minutes.
Every three-hundred-and-sixty seconds
even though they never "deserved" it
another life will pay for her sins.

Janet E. Aalfs

What Burns

We walk on a dirt road
through drying cornfields, leaves
curl green to yellow, shiver
in hot wind, damp tassels of silk shine

against blue. My friend wants to turn
around, she says, afraid
someone in a fast car will screech
up behind, stop, leap out

grab her by the hair, drag her
flailing over rocks.
She doesn't have to say who
she means. A sun scorched face

glares from a slowed down camper
like a sign marked:
Whites Only—words that now
hidden under layers of paint

still smolder, burning everyone.

Janet E. Aalfs

Worn Out

You eat hotdogs
for Christmas! she hollers
from her steps, hunched

in a dingy cable knit.
Mad at me
for having a father.

But she doesn't see
bruises the shapes of hands
he leaves.

Mad when we drive away
to the beach, come back
ice cream cones dripping.

Mad because she is
bigger and older
than me, her breasts
already sore. She yells

across the street: No
one wants to be
your friend! I see

she loves that
sweater her mother
who works all the time
knit for her, sagging
everywhere. I see through her

sweater those full
breasts like the Barbie
she lets me play
with on her porch saying
she's not mad anymore.

Then she laughs
at me for having nothing
on my chest, spits this
porch is mine,
Get off! I grab
her sleeve and yank
fierce. She twists
her ankle, falls trying
to scratch me, my fingers
clenched in soft wool.

Janet E. Aalfs

Storm Clouds

Outside Arnold's Pharmacy, sun
melted our ice cream cones
and a tough boy
we didn't know
punched my brother's face.

Out of the blue like the time our father
slammed the back door so hard
glass flew, difficult to breathe
that brittle air, no words
for what led to the crash. Frozen,

we couldn't move away
or forward, just stood
on the corner as storm clouds
passed over, leaving us
soaked and on fire.

In the silence that followed
leaves shivered a blaze of green,
and no one was there
to save us, trees shaking
droplets of light on our heads.

Ruth Margraff

The State of Gristle (a bully performance poem)

". . . the haunting of bullies last so long even deep in the muscles of now. I remember a girl who used to pull me around by my hair when I was about six. I would watch all the faces above me going by and think about wheat pennies."—*Excerpt from an e-mail from Ruth Margraff*

BABYSITTER and BOYFRIEND stroll around the stage in a circle holding hands or necking here and there to KISS songs like "Beth" or "Christine Sixteen." They stop the stroll full front behind the CPR doll which is on a baby blanket. Audio of mothers calling in the neighborhood. Lights up full bright, GIANT comes out, climbs up scaffolding, FREDA goes to her guitar. Fade to FREDA in her maxi skirt, in her doorway, trying to remember how the song goes on her guitar:

FREDA
Life was filled with guns and wars
and everyone got trampled to the floor
I wish we'd all been ready
Children died, the days grew cold
a piece of bread could buy a bag of gold
I wish we'd all been ready

Lights fade out on FREDA.

BABYSITTER jumps up into an umbrella and hangs there like Mary Poppins. Seventies folk song by Larry Norman usually coupled with Christian horror films about the Rapture or Second Coming of Christ wherein latter day believers will vanish into heaven and seven years of tribulation atrocities would follow.

2
BABYSITTER
I was absent probably. And you don't know where I am. Somebody marks it down "I think she's absent." And I flew around inside my absent place,

up past the top bar of the swingset. Somebody comes up to a screen door yellin for me, hey, come here, come back, where ya goin, but I'm absent. I get dressed to go and then I end up absent on the way, I'm gone. I call in sick, make up excuses but in the summers I mostly babysit. (*Jumps down to the CPR doll.*)

BABYSITTER
Okay so what's this Baby Wet & Wipe or Baby Wannawalk, Baby Tender Love—Baby Shivers cause it shivers till you pick it up and that screws up the batteries. I pulled all their little strings and brushed them. I know about the tube that runs down from the plastic lips so it can pee whatever, Koolaid. I know if you throw a baby in the deep end of the pool even two days old until a certain age it'll swim. Or drag it by its hair across the room, it'll think about wheat pennies. Or if it falls out of a window six stories up it'll just bounce back because it doesn't have bones yet, it's in the state of gristle, it'll still grow up, no matter what.

GIANT
On his scaffolding
But the very hairs of your head are all numbered.

A grid of longhair rises from the sanctuary, swings back and forth, singing soprano to an organ. GIANT sways inside the "stained glass" dome that is the GIANT's church.

GIANT
There shall come the longhaired ladies every Sunday with their husbands stayed at home, to keep their bald eye on the ball, good eye, good eye, Upon this rock "Be still," I built this church at 10 o'clock. I pray for them ole widow ladies wrapped in foil, God, please stick em in their tupperware and keep'em sick, and keep a blessing on each pretty hair, each pretty long hair, that gets loose with all the singin and swayin on Sunday, keep me fallin down and sweepin at it later, preachin at it, til it curls up in my dust pan

3
The longhair is raptured into the dome, leaving a few blue or red hairs in the dustpan for the GIANT.

BABYSITTER
Oh yeah but you. Hey Big Guy. Take one crazy step, you're gonna pop wide open like a blister. *(Gets the baby)* and if you fall on top of anything I'll bite you in the steeple, I won't spit it out, and take it to the cops.

GIANT
Hey little girl.

BABYSITTER
No way.

GIANT
Would you come help me sweep the church on Saturdays?

BABYSITTER
I don't think so, Big Foot.

GIANT
For a dollar? Hold the dustpan for me?

BABYSITTER
That's supposed to get dumped in the trash, you know, and I'm not standing there, cryin over ladies hairballs with ya, I am not. So just forget it.

GIANT
Sometimes they get caught on something like a nail or a hymnal or they fall down naturally, hair by hair.
(he pulls a long hair out of his mouth at some point)
And I see you have a little helper there, hello, you gonna be a fire man? Toot toot.

BABYSITTER
He's gonna go to Hell, oh God, he wants to, he says "Hell, hell, hell."

GIANT
Who says Hell?

4
BABYSITTER
"Hell, hell." Shut your dirty mouth.
(starts beating on the baby for saying hell)

GIANT *(preaching at the baby)*
That's a big word for a baby. Not a funny word, it's not a knock-knock riddle, but people keep on snickering themselves to Hell. Well what's so funny? is my question. Naked people popping pills? I met a happy Hippie on the road and I asked "What's so funny?" And the Hippie laid there for an hour laughing at my dome, this dome right here.

GIANT
in God's house. The Dome was funny, it was deep and tall and full of colors, so the Hippie laughed, ha ha ha. But oh Dear Hippie, what's so funny? Are you ready for the even Bigger Elevator Rapture? God said Lot get out of Sodom & Gomorrah I am gonna burn it to a crisp. But lo, that Lot was married to a Hippie Wife. She turned her head and I was at a rummage sale and I saw that somebody carved Lot and his wife out of ceramics. Lot was the pepper, his wife was the salt. And I smashed them both to smithereens.

BABYSITTER
(having swept some hair up) Gimme a dollar.

FREDA
(at screen door) Goddamit.

BABYSITTER
Freda says Godammit.
(runs back to FREDA)

FREDA
(to the giant)
Yeah you all got one big sermon and the rest of it is just to freak us out. I know all about the Rapture. All that rapture stuff. Twinkling of an eye. Thief in the night. Caught up together to meet the Lord in the air and so

shall they ever be with the Lord. That still happens to me sometimes. They just gotta keep you constantly on your guard . . . The King is coming. I know all the songs. I don't want my baby over there.

5
BABYSITTER
It's okay, we got a dollar, that's all.

FREDA
I don't like it, I don't like that man.

BABYSITTER
I just told the baby he's a monster, he likes monsters.
(to the baby) Rraaa.

FREDA
I don't like him liking monsters

BABYSITTER
There he goes, he's sleepin like a rock.

FREDA
(quieter) When I was in the second grade somebody gave me a picture of Jesus and it was wallet size and cut a little crooked like a school picture so the whole year I thought it was a school picture and Jesus was in the second grade but he was absent every single day. That's the kind've thing.

GIANT
Are not two sparrows sold for a farthing? and one of them shall not fall on the ground without your Father.

FREDA
Godammit

BABYSITTER
Freda says godammit I've been through the sixties twice.

FREDA

(at a screen door to the GIANT)

I've been a Hippie in a mini skirt and a Hippie in a maxi skirt. This guy never saw a maxi skirt before, he's gotta bitch about the Hippies. Yeah well, the maxi skirt means you did get Jesus at one time and then you don't got Jesus maybe but this guy—this guy just never gets out of his pulpit. Yeah, he'd pitch me into Hell but I know all the songs. I didn't forget a thing.

FREDA gets out her guitar and strums. GIANT keeps on reading out loud and mumbling.

6

FREDA

"Man and wife asleep in bed
She hears a noise and turns her head He's gone
I wish we'd all been ready
There's no time to change your mind
How could you have been so blind
The Father spoke, The demons died, The Son has come And you've been left behind." . . . Yeah I've been left behind. I lose. I'm gonna fry like bacon.

FREDA puts down her guitar and leaves.
GIANT climbs down the scaffolding to the BABYSITTER who's sweeping up the hair, the hair is stain-glassed colored now and has gotten longer.

GIANT

I pray for a wife. I've been a loner all my life. But I pray. For a wife. And I think maybe there's some places that a wife would like that I know of. Some places she'd look pretty in with stained glass windows shining on her and I'd tell people what she said like if she looked up there and said "Oh that looks like colored candy" and I'd say and then I'd tell my wife well go ahead and lick it, sometimes I lick things in the church, and I could lift her up there to the dome or if she prayed she could be lifted up there by the spirit and just fly around up there breathing up the blue air where the spirit is. In the dome. I think my wife would like the dome. And my wife would have a singing voice and I'd say my wife has a singing voice and oh my wife is in the car, she's out there in the car, my wife likes pie, my wife can't stand this weather one more minute, oh I'd like to thank my wife for . . . something, this is my wife. This is my wife, my wife made that out of stockings . ... . And one time my wife. My wife left something on the top of our car and we drove off, we didn't even know it, but it stayed up there. The whole time.

GIANT gives BABYSITTER another dollar and finishes the sweeping of the red and blue hair. BABYSITTER lays in the rest of the hair .

7
FREDA comes out with a dishpan of suds. Audio of mothers calling in the neighborhood. FREDA plays in the water acting like she's blind and gropes around for her baby to get in the bath.

FREDA
Oh I'm stirring up the soup oh boy where is my rascal for
my soup? I bet I hear a rascal over there,
(she reaches)
right there?
(reaches)
right there?
(reaches)
I smell a rascal for my soup, come on, come here, come
here, I gotcha, gonna getcha . . .

runs offstage like she is after the baby
BABYSITTER jumps up into the umbrella with the baby, they swing like
Mary Poppins

BABYSITTER
You my little sweetheart? yeah, you sugar, honey, shhhhh. You're mine, my little sweetie pie, shhhh, I love you, don't cry. You stop crying when I pick you up, I'm holding ya, I gotcha. Shhhh. You wanta kiss me, sleepy boy, you tellin me a secret, oh boy so sleepy, say "Come in," I say " Come in." somebody comes in and feeds me. MMMMmmmm, you hungry? Yeah it's nice. It's really good. So I stop crying and I'm really good. Okay you love

me, okay, love me. From the beginning. You're a big boy, yeah you gonna love me yeah, forever? Ever and ever yeah. That's all you remember. (kisses baby on the mouth) I'll show you things to remember. I take my boyfriend. I take my boyfriend to the park. Look at the most beautiful flower garden. I show my boyfriend where they tie the poodles up on their backs and clip them really round and paint their nails bright red and tie bells on their heads. I'll show you the bridge.

She pulls up her shirt and lowers down her breast onto the baby, rocks against it too tight.

BABYSITTER
I love you so much.

8
BOYFRIEND comes out and stands behind the BABYSITTER, she looks at him and gets up. BOYFRIEND goes out of the room.

BABYSITTER
And then . . . sometimes Freda just acts like my girlfriends *(FREDA comes back younger)* and she's my age and she steals my boyfriends.

FREDA takes the baby and she leans her head back and she blinks and flirts with everyone sings stuff like "Say Say oh playmate Come out and play with me." FREDA and the BABYSITTER do a dance with the doll between them and throwing it back and forth. BABYSITTER barely catches doll, FREDA circles her.

BABYSITTER
Which is my favorite song about my girlfriends. So we do all of it and then I go, Oops, when she's not looking *(drops the baby)* When she's going on back to the house.

FREDA
I'm thirsty.

BABYSITTER

Because she's thirsty and I'm really really sorry. Oh my God. Because her baby falls in the puddle and then I've gotta wash it off before she sees it like this. So I run the whole way home and sneak down underneath the house down to the basement and I wash it in the sink down there. I wash it and I'm very, very sorry and I can't believe it happened. I wish it never happened. *(She washes doll in FREDA's suds. FREDA comes back in and watches her.)* Say say oh playmate/ Come out and play with me / and bring your dolly sweet / climb up the apple tree / slide down the rain barrel / into the cellar door / and we'll be jolly friends / forever more, more, more.

9

BABYSITTER

But she's not mad about it.

FREDA takes the baby and rocks it in a blanket. Goes back to her doorway.

FREDA

I know it's late. I was just thinkin. I used to be so nervous. Yeah. When I was watching these two kids. And they were pretty good. And the one was swinging, you know—I took them to church with me, of course. There was a little swing-set in the back. And I just turned my head one second, that's the whole cliché, you know, "I turned my head one second and the baby was in the pool completely blue." I mean—well, the one was swinging ("being have" she was so cute, "I'm being have" you know) and the little one walked in front and she got hit by the—by the swing and she landed on her lip. The tooth went through it and it bled. And bled. And bled and bled. I just. I went hysterical, you know. I didn't think a baby had so much blood in one little lip and I just got it everywhere, all over in that church, the sink, all of it. But the worst part was just sitting on that couch. Somebody else's house. Waiting for the parents to get home. The kids were sleeping. I just sat there, practicing the conversation. Were they good? Yes they were good. They ate their food, they didn't fight and then. What do you say? You try. You try to watch out for the stairs and the burners and knives and keep the poison way up behind something. Keep the rugs flat. Tell them not to run so fast, don't rub that in your eye, don't squeeze the dog, don't go out in the street, just stay completely out of the street, you try to think of every sharp edge in the house that they could break their heads open on, every little object they could stick in their mouth and choke to death on. And you really really really try your best. But still.

FREDA rocks the baby.
BABYSITTER says nothing.

Well the kitchen looks fantastic, way down to the shine.
(rocks the baby) There he goes. Sleepin like a rock.

Lights fade.

10
GIANT climbs back up on the scaffolding and starts the service. Grid of longhair comes back humming, swaying slightly.

GIANT
Are not two sparrows sold for a farthing? And one of them shall not fall on the ground without your Father. But the very hairs of your head are all numbered.

Sound of a lightning bolt service stops.
FREDA comes in dripping wet and with her baby in a dresser drawer.

FREDA *(to audience as congregation, hysterical)*
Why are you here NOW? All of you are in here. Oh my God, Oh my God, I thought it happened. I've been crying for an hour. I didn't hear a thing . . . it was silent . . . all night . . . it was silent and I laid there in my bed and then at 10:00 this morning. My clock said 10:00 A.M. and I got up and I looked out the window at the church and it was empty and the street was empty and nobody's cars were moving. Nobody was out there and nobody in the house and everyone was gone. And it's Sunday. No, no, I know it's Sunday I STILL BELIEVE IN THIS. I still believe in this Rapture. I still believe in it and I think this is it. The Rapture, but it's daylight savings time and my baby's gone. I thought my baby—maybe that my baby went to heaven but I don't know, I found my baby in the house and I don't know if it was asleep

or if the Rapture maybe—or if they would leave the body on the earth like this or take the whole thing up there? I don't know the answers. I don't know. *(She goes to GIANT)* I thought I'd just come here. Just go over there, I said Okay, I'll just go over there and see if they're still here. If they're still on the earth and then I'll still be here and it'll just be daylight savings time, it would be okay.

She climbs the scaffolding in her skirt with the drawer and baby.

Then I would be okay.
(lays the drawer down at the giant's feet)
I'm fine. I'm fine. I'm fine.

Lays down on top of it still saying she's fine. Lights fade on them.

11
BOYFRIEND comes out, walks hand-in-hand with BABYSITTER as she talks.

BABYSITTER
So now my boyfriend's got a job unloading really heavy things and it's dangerous because this guy *(he knows this guy)* gets out of the truck to see how far it's backing up and the guy gets run over. Bang. They asked my boyfriend, did the guy die instantly or was it an hour later or whatever for the pain and suffering, Did the dead guy say anything, any moans or pain and suffering and then. *(BOYFRIEND walks away)* My boyfriend can't remember. He can't remember if it was really actually a word. What. What? *(She looks around for BOYFRIEND)*

He does this all the time. My boyfriend leaves the room when I am talking to him. Or I'm talking to somebody and he's sleeping in the back seat of the car and I tell the person not to wake him up, you know, because he's tired and it'll be an hour later and I'll turn around to see what kind of car is passing us *(BOYFRIEND comes back in)* and the headlights are going through the windows one by one and he's sitting straight up, he's been sitting straight up for Idon't know how long. I don't know what he remembers. And I tell him don't DO that. *(She jumps up in the umbrella.)* Please don't do that. Don't ever do that to me. Why is he doing that to me? Why is he doing that to me? Please.

BABYSITTER is lifted up and raptured into the dome with her umbrella. BOYFRIEND watches her go.

END OF PLAY

Post-show music "Walking With Jesus" By Spacemen 3

LaDonna J. Olanyk

Lunch Time Bullying

I hate it when it's lunchtime and I have to leave the room.
I follow all the others down the hall.
The teachers, they just smile at me. "He's timid," they assume.
But they don't understand it, not at all.

I sit alone and take my food out of a paper sack.
I can't afford to buy the lunch at school.
I try to eat it up real fast, before they can attack.
Sometimes the things they do are really cruel.

Some of the kids just giggle or they point and call me names.
I hate it, but that's sometimes what they do.
But what I hate the most is when they want to play their "games"
And try to tell me things I know aren't true.

"Hey Bobby, did you know I saw your grandma Tuesday night?
She dug down in a trash can for your food!"
The things they say upset me, but they know that I won't fight.
"That slop you got has already been chewed!"

I try to move away, but now they've gathered all around.
They take my food and drop it on the floor.
I watch them as they stomp it, but I never make a sound.
The bell rings and they head out for the door.

My lunch is gone. I'm hungry. I just want to sit and cry.
I wish I knew a way to make them pay.
But nothing ever changes, so I simply heave a sigh
And hope tomorrow is a better day.

Lisa Aronson Fontes

I Was Not a Bully, Truly

I was not a bully—really I wasn't. In fact, I was more often the target of teasing. I had curly hair and eyeglasses. I was the only Jew and at 10, I was a year younger than most of the girls on my block. I was a nerd, not a bully. The more popular girls called me Curly-Tops. They called me Four Eyes. They came to my house to eat popsicles and then left hastily without asking me to join them outside to play. "Next time" they told me every time. I was grateful for their visits, even if it was my desserts they wanted, not my friendship.

I agreed eagerly one day when Nancy and Jennie asked me to join them outside. We leaned against a big rock as they told me their plan. They wanted me to help them play a trick on Evie, a girl who was a baby at 9, with red hair and a Southern accent. I must have sensed that I would be one of the gang if I hurt someone who was even more "outside" than me. I would belong to the group. The excitement welled up in me.

They chose me to call Evie, since I was the only one who had ever remotely been her friend.

"Hi Evie, this is Lisa." I tried to sound casual.

"Hi Lisa! Nancy and Jennie are here. We've just started a new club. If you want to join, you've got to come over right away and get initiated."

The poison ivy was snaking up the old oak tree behind my house. Nancy, who said she wasn't allergic to poison ivy, said she would pick a leaf for Evie and show her that it was safe to touch. We planned to tell Evie that the leaf was a kind of mint, and that she had to chew on it to belong to our secret club. That there was no such club made us feel even more cunning and devious.

Evie arrived breathless, with sweat beading in her hated red hair. Never before summoned by this group of older girls, Evie was happy. Her happiness only made her look smaller and more contemptible in our eyes. Jennie, Nancy and I traded glances—we were ready to begin.

My brother, Eric, suddenly strode up waving his arms, and shouted for us to stop. He revealed the plan to Evie, who turned red between her freckles and ran home crying. The dread and guilt weighed over us like a wet sleeping bag. We could not devise an explanation that would make us look less to blame. Evie's parents told our parents. Jennie was grounded for a week. Nancy was grounded for a day. My parents told me how deeply disappointed they were in me—punishment enough.

Would I have gone through with this act of cruelty? I like to think not, but who knows? I thirsted to belong, to be "up" rather than 'down" and "in" rather than "out." Soon after, Evie and her family moved back to Alabama from whence they came. Maybe Evie remembers me as a friend. Maybe she remembers me as a bully. Maybe she does not remember this incident at all. I remember the thrill, the fear, and the shame. They all itch in me still, almost 40 years later, like poison ivy in the throat.

Susan Cleveland

The Biggest Bully

I was maybe eleven or twelve
But I still remember it well
When all the kids in the neighborhood
Surrounded me, till in the middle I stood.
I thought they'd just bury me right there
And even though I knew this was not fair
What happened next I will never forget
As I was caught up in the bully's net.
This older boy came and joined me there
I could feel the fear of danger in the air
I knew him well for he'd beaten me before
So, I began to brace myself for more.
I knew the projects were bad and scary
But I didn't know how much until my mom stepped in
She grabbed that kid, arms behind his back
And yelled at me to hit him, while she held him fast.
But because a bully I would not be
I told her "no, that's not me."
My mother turned and slapped me
Hard across my face, for all to see
Because I had embarrassed her, it's true
She became the biggest bully I ever knew.

Arjuna Greist

Bad Little Soldier

"This is a song I wrote after the Columbine massacre, linking my own experiences of being bullied in school with the culture of violence in the classroom and our society at large."—Arjuna Greist

bad little soldier
snow falls off the cars to dance a brief ballet on the grey concrete
before crushing to water under the tires of the next car in line
seething with the traffic on christopher columbus highway
all the bumps seem to me bodies bulldozed underneath
now there's tragedy on the radio, a story breaking like hearts or like bones
how can we fix this, we already know it was built wrong from the start
i'm remembering a girl with band-aids on both knees
surrounded by soldiers, marching obediently in 4/4 time
she's spinning in circles, bad little soldier
humming her own tune, disrupting the line
this isn't what the factory owners had in mind when they founded the
    schools
they wanted the upcoming workforce well-versed
in reading instructions and following rules
in history its names & dates from patriotic wars
she learns her heroes should be men who killed for more & more & more
& lessons from the dancer on the poster on the wall
pink satin shoes hide bloody scabs, she never falls from grace
she learns the most from games in gym, gotta run fast and always win
careful who you let on your team- the fittest survive,
that's how it's always been
questions quivering, strapped down in multiple choice
she's a voice muffled, trapped like an insect in amber
mouth stuffed full of sugary yellow crude rubber they tell her is gold
black and blue and red all over
out in the schoolyard she learns she is odd
then she grows older and hears on the news
how some kids tried to crawl out through a bullet hole

oh, there but for the grace of god
so i just keep driving, listening to talking heads talk, and talk,
but they never say
that 'til we stop teaching that hate is ok
the sticks and the stones won't just go away
the ship has been sinking for thousands of years
still the band keeps on playing, invading our ears
with the same tired tempo, the same keeping time
it's time to bring in a different drummer
laying down counter-point and odd numbers
a rhythm for kissing and dancing the blood off our hands
to the tune of america changing its lesson plan

Ameer Kim El-Mallawany

Playing Chicken

i do not pay the year-old
parking tickets in my drawer
as a sort of spite toward
this corner of america

where pretty zombies have a
destination, walk in pairs
down the sidewalk and will not
break stride to let you pass

Li Yun Alvarado

I Tease Your Momma 'Cause She's Fat and on Welfare

Fat is fat and welfare—
well, I don't know

what welfare is
but I know it ain't good.

You think you're cute?
With your mushroom head

and your freckled face?
You're just a momma's baby!

Everyone needs an enemy
and there's only room for one

teacher's pet in the fourth grade.
This is all I have. You welfare,

boy cut, teeny tiny bitch
ain't better than me.

Go ahead. Tell your fat Momma
I said so. No one's gonna be friends

with a stupid little tattle tale anyway.
Right everyone? Before they agree

you walk away, eyes studying
the floor in front of you. I laugh

and prepare to beat you again
at the Awards Assembly.

First honors will be mine
and I will look better than you.

After school, Abuela and I shop
for a new dress at our favorite store.
Racks and racks line each wall.
When I was younger, I would get lost

beneath the clothes or would hide
behind the dusty furniture in the back.

It always smelled like old Doña Lucy's house,
yummy, like bread and moth balls.

Abuela and I pick out a dark pink sweater dress
with black stripes along the collar and sleeves.

At home, she gives me Ritz crackers
with squares cut from our block of cheese,

then helps me manage my business. I add
thirty-five cents onto my profits column

for the seven empty cans and bottles
we collected on the way home.

At the Awards Assembly, you brag
because your ears are newly pierced

(my ears have been pierced since I was a baby).
I didn't know you could buy earrings

with food stamps! I snap and know I've won
when everybody laughs.

You don't cry. You just look at me
as if you know something I don't.

(Unlikely. I am the smart one here.)
Where did you get your dress?

you ask. And with the best
"you pathetic little bitch"

voice that I can muster, I respond:
At Salvation Army!
Everybody laughs.

Sara Littlecrow-Russell

Late, Again . . .

"You're late to every meeting!" she snarled.

With the smugness of a puritanical goodwife
Who just screamed "Witch!"
She waited for the watchers
To pelt me with rocks and garbage
To brand my forehead with a scarlet L
To light a bonfire at my feet.

But rocks, garbage, and fire were not forthcoming
(perhaps the others were unconvinced of my occult practices?)
So she pressed her Board firmly against my chest
Adding accusations like Salem stones:

Treason by diversity!

Assault by cultural difference!

Conspiracy to commit homicide!

She demanded confession
But I chose death by suffocation—
Sole dissenter drowning
In a luke-warm sea
Of their unanimous votes.

Giles Corey was one of the victims of the Salem Witch Trials. He refused to stand trial as a witch and was slowly suffocated beneath a heavy board to which large stones were periodically added in an attempt to extract his confession. The weight was such that it "forced his tongue from between his teeth" necessitating that the local sheriff use his cane to "force it in again." His excruciating death took two days.

Throughout the terror-filled year of 1692, more than other 19 innocent people were hanged because they had the misfortune to be labeled as "witches" often due to their being "different" or "disagreeable."

Albert Bermel

The Mountain Chorus: A One-Act Farce (1982)

NIGEL
DOROTHY
HACKER
SIMP
FONEY
LASSIE
SHEILA

SCENE: A mountaintop; the present.
NIGEL enters leaning into the wind, heavily laden, wearing a climbing
    outfit. He unstraps a pack from his back.

NIGEL: Dorothy, can you make it?
DOROTHY'S VOICE: I'm trying.
NIGEL: Brave girl. This looks like it. I'll check. (He takes triangulation
    equipment from his pack and surveys the site.) Pretty near perfect.
    Look at that tree. Who could ask for more? On top of a mountain . . .
    (He unfastens his pack. DOROTHY staggers in.)
DOROTHY: Finally.
NIGEL: Exactly what we hoped for. You're not too pooped?
DOROTHY: Only slightly.
NIGEL: Shall I disengage you from your pack?
DOROTHY: Bless you, Nigel.
NIGEL: Worth the climb, eh?
DOROTHY: Mm.
NIGEL: There you are. Away with the ballast. No, don't sit on your pack.
DOROTHY: I sort of folded.
NIGEL: You'll squash something. (Lays a handkerchief on the ground for
    her.) How's that?
DOROTHY: Homey.
NIGEL: Happy birthday.
DOROTHY: Thank you. Coming here was sheer inspiration.
NIGEL: I can't take all the credit.

DOROTHY: Thank you.

NIGEL: Fine place to revive the old bliss.

DOROTHY: Oh, Nigel.

NIGEL: And a tree to ourselves. A darn good tree. Pine, maybe.

DOROTHY: Gorgeous.

NIGEL: Sort of a windbreak, too. Bring the binocs?

DOROTHY: In your pack.

NIGEL: No, yours.

DOROTHY: Excuse me, Nigel.

NIGEL: You didn't forget them?

DOROTHY: Wasn't my responsibility.

NIGEL: Let's not bicker about responsibilities.

DOROTHY: Please, Nigel. On my birthday.

NIGEL: Well, dammit, we need the binocs. How will we know we're alone?

DOROTHY: Here they are. In my pack.

NIGEL. Ha. (He takes them from her.)

DOROTHY: Nigel.

NIGEL: What are you worried about now?

DOROTHY: Love me?

NIGEL: Love you. And me?

DOROTHY: You too. Yes, much.

NIGEL: (Using the binoculars) Well and truly alone. All those other mountains. But miles away. Swarming with tourists. Wanted to make sure. Now I'll see about the tent.

DOROTHY: Will it be out of sight of the other mountains?

NIGEL: In the hollow here. (He begins to erect the tent.)

DOROTHY: But from the air? Planes and so forth?

NIGEL: Sturdy fabric. Very opaque. I asked the salesman.

DOROTHY: Don't you want a drink first?

NIGEL: Later.

DOROTHY: Even a little one?

NIGEL: I said later.

DOROTHY: Nigel.

NIGEL: What now?

DOROTHY: Love me?

NIGEL: Love you.

DOROTHY: And . . . ?

NIGEL: And me?

DOROTHY: You, too.

NIGEL: Damn awkward with this wind.

DOROTHY: Can I help?

NIGEL: No. It's your birthday.

DOROTHY: It's a pretty tent.

NIGEL: If you say so.

DOROTHY: Expensive?

NIGEL: Nothing's too expensive for your birthday.

DOROTHY: Thank you.

NIGEL: Blast the wind. And the ground is solid rock. How do they expect you to put up a tent in a place like this?

DOROTHY: Leave it till later.

NIGEL: I will not. Tent's the first thing we need. If a tree can stand here, so can a tent.

DOROTHY: Unroll the mattresses?

NIGEL: If you like.

DOROTHY: I brought the blue sheets with the pattern. Not the white ones. And the blue pillowcases.

NIGEL: Why the blue?

DOROTHY: Matches the top of the mountain.

NIGEL: There it is. Our tent.

DOROTHY: Stunning.

NIGEL: Oh . . .

DOROTHY: Nigel, what is it?

NIGEL: Should've made up the beds first. How are we going to fix them inside that dinky little tent?

DOROTHY: I'll do it.

NIGEL: You'll knock the tent over.

DOROTHY: No, I'm careful with tents.

NIGEL: Forget it. (He takes the mattresses and slides them into the tent.)

DOROTHY: I'll be fixing the drinks.

NIGEL: My job.

DOROTHY: I want to be useful.

NIGEL: Chill the glasses.

DOROTHY: Where's the insulated bag?

NIGEL: Your pack. Top left compartment.

DOROTHY: Do we have enough ice?

NIGEL: We're strong on cubes. Not sure about the crushed. (Pause) The beds just about fit.

DOROTHY: Goody.

NIGEL: Which way do our heads go? If we put them next to the entrance flap we'll catch a draught. If we have them at the other end, how will we ever get in?

DOROTHY: I'm for lots of breeze. These winds stimulate me. Glass chilled enough?

NIGEL: Next to my cheek, please.

DOROTHY: Yes?

NIGEL: Could be a mite cooler. There are the beds. Not the most thrilling bed-making job I've ever seen, but sleepable.

DOROTHY: Nigel, they're darling.

NIGEL: Now for the rug. (He spreads it out in front of the tent.)

DOROTHY: Nigel, a white fur rug.

NIGEL: For the, you know, preliminaries.

DOROTHY: How considerate. Where did you get it?

NIGEL: Sporting goods store.

DOROTHY: Real fur?

NIGEL: Imitation polar bear. Washable. Static-free.

DOROTHY: It's all gruff and grumpy. I love it.

NIGEL: What next? The banner.

DOROTHY: Yes, please. Nigel, why don't we . . . ?

NIGEL: What?

DOROTHY: Put it on the tree.

NIGEL: Let me think. Yes, the tree would work. (He takes out a college banner and nails it to the tree.)

DOROTHY: The tree suits it.

NIGEL: What about the suntan oil?

DOROTHY: I brought lotion. Didn't want to grease up the sheets. But Nigel, you're not sunbathing in this wind?

NIGEL: Might get a windburn.

DOROTHY: A good point.

NIGEL: On the other hand, the sun may come out later. Time for refreshments. What're you having?

DOROTHY: What are you?

NIGEL: A vodka martini.

DOROTHY: Japalac, please.

NIGEL: One dash of raspberry syrup? Have two. It's your birthday.

DOROTHY: One and a half. Light on the rye.

NIGEL: (Mixing) How are the glasses coming along?

DOROTHY: Try.

NIGEL: Good. Keep them at that temperature.

DOROTHY: (Looking through the binoculars.) Astounding view. In every direction.

NIGEL: Very varied.

DOROTHY: Hors d'oeuvres. Caviar or whitefish dip?

NIGEL: A nibble of both.

DOROTHY: On an onion biscuit?

NIGEL: Why not?

DOROTHY: I'll risk the health pumpernickel.

NIGEL: Where's the tray? (She gives him a silver tray. He arranges the drinks and the hors d'oeuvres. He sets up stack tables and unfolds a pair of chairs. They put their drinks on coasters.)

DOROTHY: Whose toast?

NIGEL: It's your birthday.

DOROTHY: That's hard. I'm thinking. Got it. To everything.

NIGEL: I'll drink to that. (He does.)

DOROTHY: The Japalac is overpoweringly good.

NIGEL: The raspberry syrup. I put in one and three quarters.

DOROTHY: Nigel, you shouldn't've.

NIGEL: The caviar isn't bad.

DOROTHY: Nor is the whitefish.

NIGEL: Another toast?

DOROTHY: Interesting idea. Your turn.

NIGEL: To a successful conclusion.

DOROTHY: Nigel, you're so risqué.

NIGEL: Oh.

DOROTHY: What?

NIGEL: A mark on the silverware.

DOROTHY: Tarnish?

NIGEL: Looks like it.

DOROTHY: Borrow mine.

NIGEL: It doesn't matter.

DOROTHY: Not quite hygienic. But my lipstick has practically worn off.

NIGEL: I said it doesn't matter.

DOROTHY: Nigel.

NIGEL: Yes?

DOROTHY: Love me?

NIGEL: Love you.

DOROTHY: You forgot again.

NIGEL: And me?

DOROTHY: You too. Nigel, this is heaven.

NIGEL: Thank you. Must keep up with the sexual revolution.

DOROTHY: The what?

NIGEL: You know, the younger generation.

DOROTHY: It's better than our honeymoon.

NIGEL: Higher up, anyway.

DOROTHY: Remember that Bermuda beach hut where you . . . ?

NIGEL: I could really wear swim shorts.

DOROTHY: Nigel, you're awfully preserved.

NIGEL: Thank you. I'll get out the transformer.

DOROTHY: Nigel, shouldn't we . . . ?

NIGEL: What?

DOROTHY: Be at it.

NIGEL: Must get in the mood first. Radio or TV?

DOROTHY: TV, please. More to look at. (He takes out a portable set and twiddles.) Oh, dear. Nothing but soap opera.

NIGEL: We'll try the stereo.

DOROTHY: No, leave this on. Something to look at.

NIGEL: Contrast is only so-so. Brightness not much better.

DOROTHY: One of those other mountains getting in the way?

NIGEL: Impossible. This is a mountaintop model.

DOROTHY: They think of everything.

NIGEL: For a price.

DOROTHY: Can you up the sound?

NIGEL: On full already. Better hook up the stereo. We ought to get plenty of dimensional resonance with the valley down there, the sky up there.

DOROTHY: There's a beautiful cloud.

NIGEL: Don't see it.

DOROTHY: Behind the TV antenna.

NIGEL: Nasty-looking fellow.

DOROTHY: Has a head like a unicorn. Would you refresh my Japalac?

NIGEL: Must clear up this wiring first. You got the leads from the pre-amp tangled in your pack with the audio cable. (DOROTHY helps herself to another drink.)

DOROTHY: That unicorn. It has two horns.

NIGEL: If the transformer's not in shape, we're sunk. I wouldn't be surprised if the connections took a hell of a jolting up that hill.

DOROTHY: Not two horns. Three. And three heads. Four, five, six, seven . . . Believe it or not.

NIGEL: For God's sake, Dorothy. Don't keep on with your horns while I'm concentrating.

DOROTHY: The next mountain on the right has a peach of a waterfall. Most exhilarating to watch. All that foam. Bunching up at the edge. Then—whoosh. Nigel, what would happen if this mountain turned into a volcano? Right underneath us? Would we be swallowed up? In boiling lava?

NIGEL: No.

DOROTHY: Why not?

NIGEL: This isn't volcano country.

DOROTHY: How can you be sure?

NIGEL: I found the red terminal.

DOROTHY: I'm having another Japalac. Nigel!

NIGEL: Go ahead. It's your birthday.

DOROTHY: I'm putting in three raspberry syrups and two ryes.

NIGEL: Where's the outlet for the black terminal? That's all I ask.

DOROTHY: Come and sit down. You're all tense on my birthday.

NIGEL: So. Now we'll see if the whole thing goes up in smoke.

DOROTHY: That would be a shame. Personally I couldn't care less.

NIGEL: Hear that? (Violinny dance music begins.) Reception's terrific. I'll move the other speaker three or four inches.

DOROTHY: Have another vodka martini.

NIGEL: Give me a couple of minutes. To unlax.

DOROTHY: Put your head in my lap.

NIGEL: I won't be able to see the screen.

DOROTHY: Turn it. (He does, then sits in the folding chair. She tries to take his head in her lap.)

NIGEL: Don't think much of the color. The folding chair is folding under me.

DOROTHY: How about this? (She lies on the white rug.)

NIGEL: Be over before long. For soap opera this is quite respectable.

DOROTHY: The unicorn cloud's gone. Surged away. Here comes its baby.

NIGEL: Unicorns are out in force today. What's happening to the stereo? The automatic frequency control must have slipped to manual. Dorothy, we're skidding between stations.

DOROTHY: It does sound weird. To hell with it.

NIGEL: And the tuner's new. Paid on the spot for it. The check's gone through by now. Should have taken out a charge account there.

DOROTHY: I think it's another radio. Somebody else coming.

NIGEL: Christ! I made sure we'd have this peak to ourselves.

DOROTHY: Snub them bitterly. Keep watching the TV. (She gets up and joins him.)

NIGEL: Why should they enjoy the privileges of our TV and stereo? Who lugged them all they way up? (NIGEL switches off the radio, turns down the television sound.) Here's a book. Read.

DOROTHY: I'm off books lately. No ads or anything.

NIGEL: The New Yorker?

DOROTHY: That's more like it. Lots of color. Nigel, they couldn't have chosen a worse time to invade us. I was getting receptive. Tell them it's my birthday. If they take the hint.

NIGEL: Won't be for long. We'll freeze them out. (The other radio approaches. Six young people appear. Four are boys: HACKER, TAPPY, SIMP, FONEY. Two are girls: SHEILA, LASSIE.)

HACKER: By the tree. (To NIGEL) Hi, Pops. (To the others) In a clean, gentleman-type circle.

TAPPY: Is this for a war council?

HACKER: Don't get brighty with me. (Hits TAPPY in the face.)

TAPPY: What did I say?

HACKER: (To SIMP, who has the radio) And cut that radio.

SIMP: I could make it like low.

HACKER: I said cut it. (Throws the radio over the edge.) A nice drop. Must be six, seven hundred feet down. Made sweet music all the way.

SIMP: But Hacker.

HACKER: I told you you wasn't to bring it. Take the roll call.

SIMP: My brother bought that radio.

HACKER: Take the roll call or your brother will have to buy a new brother. (LASSIE leans against the tree and decorates her eyes with a green pencil. FONEY necks with SHEILA.) Foney, get off that chick's chest while we're taking roll call.

DOROTHY: Are they planning to stay here?

NIGEL: If they are I'll have a stern word with them.

HACKER: Say, Pops, you don't have to breeze or nothing. Stick around with the broad.

NIGEL: This lady is my wife.

HACKER: Nice going, Pops. Simp, did I hear you not reading the roll call?

SIMP: Hacker, honorary president.

HACKER: Here.

SIMP: Simp, honorary secretary. Here. Foney, honorary treasurer.

FONEY: What? Here.

HACKER: I told you: stop chewing at that chick.

SIMP: Tappy, honorary advisory observer.

TAPPY: Here. What's all this about?

HACKER: Ask me one more question. Just one more. Okay, Mr. Secretary. Take the minutes of the last meeting.

(NIGEL stands up)

NIGEL: Pardon me. My wife and I purposely chose this isolated peak.

SIMP: This what?

HACKER: You stiff. Keep your ears ungummed. The man said, "Peak." That right, Pops: Peak?

NIGEL: And if you intend to remain here . . .

HACKER: We intend, Pops. But that don't give you no reason to blow. Is somebody hustling you? Simp, why did you quit reading?

SIMP: "The exec committee met . . ."

SHEILA: Haw.

SIMP: Shut your goddam lip.

SHEILA: Go stuff.

SIMP: Hacker, shall I give it to her?

HACKER: Mr. Secretary, I didn't like that word "goddamn." That is not a gentleman-type word. Get going with the minutes.

SIMP: I keep thinking about that sonafabitching radio.

HACKER: Any more slang like that out of you while we got company and I'll take your face apart.

SIMP: "The exec committee met in conclave at the corner table in Kuppenheimer's Drugstore & Paperback Jamboree. Present were the following Toreadors . . ."

SHEILA: Haw.

HACKER: Give it to her.

SIMP: Me?

HACKER: You. Anybody. Everybody. (The boys all strike SHEILA.)

LASSIE: You scum. Hitting a girl. What you want to do that for?

HACKER: That's not my idea of a quality-type word. Scum. Give it to her. (They strike LASSIE. She sits and weeps, the green running down her face.)

SHEILA: Foney, after that, don't you never come near me again.

FONEY: It was a little hit, baby. Here, I'll make it better.

NIGEL: I don't wish to intrude on your deliberations. I must remind you, though, that first claims come first. I expect you to honor ours.

HACKER: Sure, Pops. You sit back and make like you're in your own mansion. Simp?

SIMP: "Present were the following Toreadors from the exec committee: Hacker, Simp, Foney. Also Lassie, Sheila, and Tappy, observers . . ." Ahh . . .

NIGEL: And I don't approve of your striking girls.

HACKER: Anything you say, Pops. Simp, if you quit reading them minutes one more time you'll get my toe where you can't wear it.

SIMP: "The exec committee agreed with the honorary president that the proposed rumble between the Toreadors and their deadly foes, the Muckrakers, will, shall, and should take place as heretofore decided by the honorary president. The meeting thereupon ended."

HACKER: Who put in that word "deadly?"

SIMP: Me, I guess.

HACKER: Is that a gentleman-type word?

SIMP: I'll take it out.

HACKER: Gink. You delete it.

NIGEL: Are you ignoring my request? Perhaps I should warn you that I can enforce it. As a former fullback who has maintained his condition by climbing and other activities—

HACKER: Does anybody accept the minutes? Minutes accepted.

NIGEL: And further, as an amateur boxer of no mean prowess-

HACKER: Pops, you're the champ. So we Toreadors have to make up our executive mind why said rumble didn't take place.

FONEY: Somebody ratted.

NIGEL: Threats don't seem to deter them. Should I take action?

DOROTHY: Nigel, they're young.

TAPPY: Look, is this a war council?

HACKER: Give it to him. (The boys descend on TAPPY and strike him.) One warning out to be enough, Tappy. Now, like Foney explained, somebody ratted. Except ratted is not a quality-type word. Somebody betrayed. Some canary flew to the boys in blue and said, "The Toreadors figure to rumble." And the blue boys greased him up good. He took away all the green he could handle.

TAPPY: Don't we have no idea who done it?

HACKER: We have a very fine idea.

TAPPY: Then what?

HACKER: Then we're holding an official-type inquiry.

FONEY: Great!

HACKER: Shut your ugly-type yap.

FONEY: Maybe I want to confess.

HACKER: Yes-?

FONEY: . . . I was kidding.

HACKER: At an inquiry? (Striking him.) Do I have to keep all the order around here with my two single hands?

SHEILA: What you want to hit him for?

FONEY: Now you give me a black eye or something.

HACKER: We better level that off. (Strikes him in the other eye.) We don't want our treasurer losing his honorary balance.

LASSIE: He lost it when he come out of his mother's whatever he comes out of.

HACKER: Lassie, one more squawk and I'll hand you the straight treatment. I'm still waiting for this confession. It better fly out quick. And it better be in a clean language Toreador-type confession all the way.

NIGEL: This is intolerable.

DOROTHY: Nigel, let's move on.

NIGEL: Uproot the tent? Set up the stereo again after it's going so beautifully? I give them five minutes. After that, I boot them off this peak.

DOROTHY: They've taken over.

HACKER: (His eyes fixed on SIMP) Who's about to confess?

SIMP: (Squirming) I don't have anything to confess. Except if I confess on somebody else.

HACKER: You want to sing a song—? Point a finger? . . . That's a bad sign.

SIMP: if the guilty one don't confess I meant I'll confess on them.

HACKER: What you say to that, Foney?

FONEY: Me? It's not true.

HACKER: You never spoke to no blue boys?

FONEY: I was a gentleman-type Toreador all the way through.

HACKER: Get your hand outta her skirt when you tell me that.

FONEY: I swear on my mother's coffin.

HACKER: Your mother is alive and living.

FONEY: She's got to go into a coffin some day, don't she?

HACKER: How about Tappy there?

TAPPY: You picking on me again?

HACKER: Don't throw me a question when I throw you a question.

TAPPY: How about me? And how about you, Hacker?

HACKER: After I warned you. You threw me two questions. I'm going to push your mouth where it ought to go, down your ignorant-type throat.

NIGEL: Four minutes up.

DOROTHY: Nigel, before you explode give them fair warning. Listen to me, you boys. How long are you staying here with these games?

HACKER: Games, lady? If this is games I like to know what's for real. Right, Pops?

NIGEL: Do you mind not calling me "Pops?" I'm old enough to be your father.

FONEY: How old would that be, Pops? You must be damn near thirty.

HACKER: Foney, apologize to the old folks for that word you said there. Or I'll rub your nose out on that tree till one of them wears out.

FONEY: I apologize.

HACKER: (Turns back to NIGEL) Like I said, Pops, you can sit around.

NIGEL: I mean to, I assure you.

DOROTHY: How did you get up here?

SIMP: We come in the convertible.

NIGEL: I suggest you scramble back into your convertible and take off instantly.

DOROTHY: A road. Nigel, we may get crowded off this mountain by more hooligans. Let's pack.

HACKER: Stick around, Pops. You might see something you can tell the world.

NIGEL: Be sensible, Dorothy. We can't unmake the beds in front of these snickering infants.

HACKER: It's a straight invitation. You wouldn't want to reject me, would you, Pops?

DOROTHY: How long will you be here?

HACKER: You know how it is, lady. When you have something on your executive mind. What you do, Pops? You a lawyer? Our defendant could sure use a hot lawyer. It might shorten this inquiry up.

TAPPY: What you mean, defendant, Hacker?

HACKER: You been in plenty big law cases, Pops? The newspaper-type kind of cases?

NIGEL: I am not a lawyer.

HACKER: Okay, Pops, you're the like citizen-type.

NIGEL: Will you please refrain from calling me "Pops?"

HACKER: Refrain?

NIGEL: Yes. Desist.

HACKER: Desist, refrain, desist. Did you clunks hear them dignity-type words? Simp, you better took them down in your minutes.

SIMP: Just wrote them, Hacker.

HACKER: Pops, you certainly are the class we need around here.

DOROTHY: Nigel, don't let them provoke you.

HACKER: Look at it this way, Pops. Nobody's hanging on to you by the short hairs or nothing. You want to breeze—

NIGEL: By God, Dorothy, just step out of sight and I'll . . .

HACKER: Nothing is going to like happen, Pops. Be our guest.

NIGEL: We were here first.

HACKER: Sure you was. (Turns, ominously.) So, we come back to Tappy . . . (TAPPY starts to dash away. HACKER dives at his legs and brings him down, then sits on his head.) You slobs see how slowball you are around here? If I wasn't on the team every body would like cut out. Now, What's with Tappy? He afraid of this legal-type inquiry? Maybe he's sorry he ratted on his colleague-type buddies.

TAPPY: I didn't do nothing. You're breaking my neck.

HACKER: Tap, take it easy. All that bouncing makes me not comfortable.

NIGEL: You have no right to squash that boy's head.

HACKER: Cool it, Pops. Let's not get all busy before we investigate what this inquiry is going to prove.

TAPPY: You're killing my neck.

NIGEL: Let the boy rise and speak for himself.

HACKER: You hear that, Tappy? You got yourself a lawyer. One of the biggest. Pops here is the king of the brighty lawyers.

SIMP: Let's swing. I'm getting the chills. (He idly punches FONEY's arm. (FONEY comes out of his necking trance with SHEILA and punches back. Then beat away at each other's biceps. HACKER gets off TAPPY's head and pulls him to his feet by the collar.)

HACKER: Okay, let the inquiry roll.

NIGEL: Release that boy.

TAPPY: I didn't squeal. Not one word.

HACKER: You'll squeal plenty before this deal is through. Okay, you gentlemen of the jury. Unsuck your face from that cheap-type broad. This is big business for we Toreadors. Let's have respect for the law. Go ahead, Tappy. Spill.

NIGEL: Release him. I shan't say it again.

TAPPY: What are you going to do to me?

HACKER: Now, Tappy, could I tell you that before I knew if you was like one thousand per cent guilty or less?

TAPPY: I mean, if I was to confess on myself, would I get a reprieve-type sentence?

HACKER: What you think this jury is for? Making bargains with a prisoner? Either you confess or . . .

TAPPY: Mister, will you protect me?

NIGEL: Before I say another thing, my boy, I want you to understand that whatever you've done or have not done is hardly my concern.

DOROTHY: (Apprehensively) Nigel! Beds, banner, tent, everything . . . Come!

NIGEL: (To TAPPY) I don't envy you your fate but perhaps this incident will teach you to select thoughtful companions, not roughnecks.

HACKER: Hey, Pops, watch out for that foul-type language. Like we can lose our cool, too.

TAPPY: Crud on the lotta you. So I betrayed! You was always coming down on me. I was the youngest nobody around. Now I count. I went to the cops. I cut that rumble dead. I was on the both sides at the same time. All the world trusted me. That was pretty good, hey?

HACKER: Everybody's friend. A very sweet-type arrangement.

TAPPY: You bet your butt it was. (NIGEL steps forward. DOROTHY clutches at him.)

HACKER: And no fuzz didn't hand you no bread? No crumbs . . . ?

TAPPY: No.

FONEY: Clobber the truth out of his guts.

SIMP: I knew it was him all along.

HACKER: You see what these Toreadors are asking for, Tappy? They want a bit of your like blood. Keep them unhappy. Spit up the truth.

TAPPY: I am.

HACKER: Fix him against the tree. For a total confession. (FONEY and SIMP pin TAPPY against the tree.) And here we have a rock with kind of edges. (He presses the edge into the small of TAPPY's back.) We didn't even start yet . . . A bit of friendly pressure. Until we come to the full truth.

TAPPY: (Relenting) Okay. Okay. All the getting cut up and beat up all the time . . .

HACKER: (Ignoring TAPPY's attempted explanation) . . . Not only did you rat. You lost your respect for the decent things in life. It don't twist your insides when the Muckrakers cross up our honor?

TAPPY: Get that rock thing outta my back.

HACKER: You was afraid you might be the somebody got hurt in the rumble.

TAPPY: Not only me. (More pained.) That rock . . .

NIGEL: Dorothy, I don't want to push you aside, but . . .

HACKER: We Toreadors wouldn't destroy a colleague's backbone. Get that rope and tie him a very fine noose.

NIGEL: That's my mountain rope.

HACKER: We pay you for it, Pops.

NIGEL: To lynch him with?

HACKER: No question of a lynch. We just tie him to this strong-type tree and let him dangle his yelling tail. We wouldn't damage him. He's an associate. Except he ratted. He'll be safe as home hanging over this nature-type cliff.

TAPPY: How come it's always my buddies get cut up? Beaten? Never one of you exec committee guys for a change? The whistle blows, you're out there in the back of us.

HACKER: Hear that, Pops? That's the type criminal mind you're facing here. I mean, mean.

NIGEL: Let that boy go! (He pushes DOROTHY aside, strides over to FONEY and SIMP, and pulls their arms away. TAPPY darts behind the tree and escapes.)

HACKER: (Stalkingly) Why'd you want to do a thing like that, Pops—? (He leaps at NIGEL and knocks him to the ground. After a struggle, the boys tie NIGEL with the rope.) Pops, you're mean, like Tappy. Letting him cut out. It could waste a whole 'nother day before we capture him. We thought you was more polite . . .

DOROTHY: Take your hands off him!

HACKER: We don't use our hands, lady. This like rope does it all.

DOROTHY: It's my birthday.

HACKER: All the very best, lady, from all of us on the exec committee.

DOROTHY: You degraded young ruffians, you animals, you shit!

HACKER: I could of swore you was a gentleman-type lady. And here you bust out with them kind of personal statements.

NIGEL: You're not to lay a hand on her, you hear?

HACKER: What's all this about hands? (Holds out his hands.) Here's my hands, Pops. Not fooling with a thing. You're just too heated, Pops. (He ties the other end of the rope to the tree.) We'll just hang you out in that fresh air.

DOROTHY: He's done nothing to you!

HACKER: . . . Only let our defendant cut out. Only broke up our pro-ceedings. But we don't got a thing against old Pops . . . You interested in space, Pops?

NIGEL: Whatever you do, let my wife go! She's a woman . . .

HACKER: Oh, I seen that, Pops, all the way up and down. You know? Like my personal mother is a woman. A very refined woman. You refrain and desist, Pops. And just don't rock the rope.

NIGEL: If you touch her -?

HACKER: Shame on your snazzy head, Pops, for thinking such-type things. This isn't my age of pickle. Okay, let him sink. (FONEY and SIMP lower NIGEL over the edge. DOROTHY rushes toward him. HACKER places himself in her way. He steps forward. DOROTHY sinks down onto the ground silently, just staring blankly ahead. NIGEL's voice is heard, but not his words.)

SHEILA: Anybody would think they was feebs the way it takes the both of them to lower one poor schnook who isn't no bigger than either one of them put together.

LASSIE: Some musclemen.

SIMP: (Straining) I'll talk to you later, you hairy hooker. (He and FONEY finish letting the rope out. They stand back.)

FONEY: It's a powerful-type rope.

SIMP: A cinch.

FONEY: Hold forever. (The tree suddenly comes out of the ground and topples over the edge after NIGEL.)

LASSIE: You Toreadors forget about the thin soil around here? (DOROTHY looks up, sees the tree is missing, screams, and goes back into her stupor.)

FONEY: It was this wind must have done it.

LASSIE: You geek-type murderers! Poor old guy . . .

SHEILA: He wasn't so old . . .

FONEY: (Approaching DOROTHY) Lady, it was a accident. Right, Hacker?

HACKER: That's right, lady. The boys didn't mean a thing.

FONEY: What you mean . . . the boys?

HACKER: (Ignoring him) Listen, lady, a deal. We wouldn't let you carry him home alone in that wet state. We was like attached to old Pops. We'll bring him up here. And, if they ask you, we was the witness. We saw, see? The whole mess . . .

FONEY: Boy!

SIMP: Boy, ahoy! Wow!

FONEY: This looks like it!

HACKER: Quit the brighty talk! You two slobs was the one tied the
knots. First, we got to bring back old smashed-up Pops. Don't move
a toe, lady. We'll be up here again in one second flat, so you don't
have to be without old Pops on your birthday. (They look back at
DOROTHY. Then they run. There is the sound of their car racing
away. After a moment, DOROTHY rises and slowly crosses back to
the encampment.)

DOROTHY All this sun. So cold. Must be . . . late . . . (Then, suddenly)
Nigel! Nigel! (Weeping) And the banner. Your forlorn banner . . .
(After taking a long drink and finishing NIGEL's, she notices the
television set which is still on. She crosses to her chair and sits down,
staring blankly, and sobbing. Gradually, the television begins to
interest her.) Can't hear a thing . . . (She turns up the volume. She
continues to sob now and again. The television program takes hold
of her. She stares at it, intently. Her sobs diminish. She smiles. She
laughs . . .)

Curtain

Eilish Thompson

Mission Unaccomplished

I
Fission.
Who launches the final decision?
Division.
Causing confusion,
and combustion.
We shout: mission accomplished!

II
Nagasaki.
Hiroshima.
Your voices are caught
in the mushroom cloud exhaust.
Your protests are engulfed
by its smoke.
The residue of this nuclear disaster is spread
out over your cities,
a bittersweet dust that one cannot taste
except
when one commits murder.
The rays are echoed through the cavities of your dead bodies.
Did we shout "mission accomplished"
when our weapons invaded foreign air?

III
Russia and America—
what did you hope to gain
with threats aimed at each other
across the world, whose only answers are given in half-lives?
Perhaps the sky for a canvas—
slicked with blood and
painted with an explosion of a
nuclear disaster

too radioactive to control?
Should we shout "mission accomplished"
and salute the weapons of mass destruction
a symbol of our tyranny?

IV
Fission.
Who launches the final decision?
Division.
Causing confusion,
and combustion.
You alone cry, "mission accomplished."

Sara Littlecrow-Russell

For My Student Who Was Dangled Over the Second Floor Railing by the Young Republicans

A world upside down
Coalesced with terror's crystalline sharpness—
Pepto-Bismol colored walls
Dirt-flecked asbestos floor tiles
Sweat-slick aluminum railing
Slipped like an elusive lover beneath your grasping hands,
As the air filled with aftershave—acrid and curdled
From the oppositional chemistry of their violent arousal
And sudden, panicked understanding
That their heterosexuality is as fragile
As skin stretched across a bare knuckle.

We were instructed to ignore this,
But I have seen the microeconomics of hate—
Bones pushing through gaping flesh,
Matted hair wet and sticky with blood,
Paralyzed limbs and catheter bags
And when I climb the stairs
My hands bless the industrial hideousness
Of this rail that protected you from our failings.

Eilish Thompson

For the Victims of the Machine

Their blood is soaking through my camouflaged pants
Of this uniform I wear, and I am
Forced to conform to the care—
Less responsibility.
But such camouflage cannot hide my fear.
And the green is yet again revealed
To darken the morbid hope
Attempting to resurface through the gore
That insinuates this is glory.
The sins of their souls seeping through my sleeve and it is then
    I question:
What was their sin?
Were they defending their liberty as I sought to steal it away from them
With a perceived precision of purpose?
Were their children aware that I hid in the coldest part of the flame,
And that we hid under the shadows of shame and sin of 100,000
    innocent deaths
That went unnoticed by my leaders
Who I follow like a dog?
Their words are my bone
That I chase after because of necessity, the need to survive alone
Is enough to force us to demean ourselves and others and deplete the cells
    of our common sense,
and to devalue the lives of our sisters and brothers.
There is no convenient way to say this.
I kill anyone who gets in the way of my orders
Which I must reiterate I follow like a dog at bay.
Joe Smith is the name my dog tags will say
Jane Smith is my wife's name. And we're not average,
But that's what our tax records say.
We have to pay.

I pay in blood. My kids play in mud.
Their innocence protrudes from their eyes in the pictures they sent
And as I show my unit, someone questions
If these pictures are God-sent and hell-bent.
I fit this question in the space between my finger and the trigger
And fire.

SCHOOLS

Tell me and I'll forget;
show me and I may remember,
involve me and I'll understand.
—Chinese proverb

Eilish Thompson

Education Plans for the School Year

Pre-school pre-requisite:
All children who wish to enroll in the Pre-School of this city,
Must first pass a test in which they must follow every direction to its
    fullest extent.
Fear not, parents! This test is Nation-Wide, used in many other states,
And is proof that America is adopting the Old Chinese Method
    of Teaching—
And while some people refer to it as "Drill and Kill,"
We hope you will see the rudeness that such a phrase implies
And will therefore never say it.
We must of course set the example for our children.
Which is why, and it is our expectation that you will understand,
That it is in the best interest of this city,
And of your children's of course,
Even of yours,
To accept this, and ask no questions.
Again, we must set a proper example for the future generations to adopt.
Also, we will need from you,
Besides your child's mind to conform, transform, and mold into our
    better view,
A sample of your writing.
You see, we intend on making this city the best American city it can be,
And since we do live in America,
We will just need to be sure that you speak English well.
After all, what good would it do for this city,
To have its future learning a language and have no help at home?
We are confident that you understand.

In order to pass Kindergarten, all students must exhibit the ability to
Speak only when spoken to,
And they must be scored on a Pass/Fail scale
On their development.
If they fail to display this ability,

For example, by talking back,
By not speaking or standing during the Pledge of Allegiance,
By questioning anything their masterful teacher tells them.
After all, it is better to nip any problem in the bud
And prevent any type of nuisance to society,
Seeker of change, or radical.

In order to pass First Grade, all students must be able
To draw the American Flag,
Incorporate Learning Targets: R,W, & B.
If however, there are any students who seem to exhibit a strong pull
Towards drawing and coloring, they must be discouraged
As Art class funding has been cut completely in order to help fix the
    budget.
It is important to note that if such a problem persists,
The monies that will be needed to replenish the coloring tools
Will be extracted from the Teacher's paycheck.
Introducing complete Color-Blindness is always also an option
For those students who refuse to conform.

In order to pass the Second Grade, all students must be able
To salute with the correct hand.
Any student who is caught not saluting the school principal
Will be expelled, and charged with Defiance.
(The legal term's definition is still under construction)

Carlos David Palacio

Quinto grado, ¡mi peor pesadilla!

Todo comenzó en la maravillosa mañana del primer día de septiembre. Era mi primera vez en una escuela elemental en este país. Yo tenia once años y como nací y crecí en Latino América, como era de suponerse en ese momento yo no hablaba inglés. Recuerdo que ese primer día de escuela fue lo peor que me a pasado en la vida. Cuando entré a la clase que me asignaron, me sentí intimidado porque ninguno de mis compañeros de clase hablaba el idioma español. Gracias a esa gran intimidación, yo estaba a punto de llorar cuando en ese mismo momento una maestra que hablaba español entro por casualidad y se ofreció a ayudarme.

El comienzo del año escolar fue muy difícil, no tenía ningún amigo, no tenía nadie que me ayudara en mis tareas escolares, pero lo que hacía mi vida cada vez más difícil eran mis propios compañeros de clase que se burlaban de mi acento y de el poco inglés que yo hablaba. Mis compañeros siguieron con el mismo patrón de conducta hasta que un día me sentí tan intimidado que tomé una decisión. Tomé la decisión de hablar con mi maestro y decirle lo que me estaba pasando. Esa fue la mejor decisión que pude haber tomado y desde ese momento mi vida cambió completamente.

Carlos David Palacio

Fifth Grade, My Worst Nightmare
(translated by María Luisa Arroyo)

It all began on a marvelous first day of September. It was my first day in elementary school in this country. I was eleven years old, and since I was born and raised in Latin America, at that time I did not speak English. I remember that first school day as the worst day of my life. When I went to my assigned class, I felt intimidated because none of my classmates spoke Spanish. I felt intimidated to the point of tears. At that moment a teacher who spoke Spanish happened to come by and offered to help me.

The beginning of the school year was very difficult. I had no friends, I had no one to help me with assignments, but what made it worse, was that my classmates made fun of my accent and the little English that I spoke. My classmates kept taunting me, until I made a decision. I decided to speak with my teacher about it and tell him what was happening to me. That was the best decision I could have made, and my life changed completely.

Ameer Kim El-Mallawany

Fatimata

The lifeless stone gargoyle that
Guards the shadowy backdoor to my soul
Reminds me of you
Whom I have never seen—

The legend (key in weathered rock-hand):

How did you become the abused earth-mother
Or did they trod over your flesh with insolent shoes and
Peruse their reflections in those sole-less
Footprints frozen over by their icicle eyes
And hate what they saw,
Blame you?

The statue has a voice like
I imagine yours to be
Your name bounces off the fogged
Windows of the yellow school bus in my mind
And sounds like the fickle laughter of rootless white children.
They have made it so, Fatimata
Martyr.
I cannot hear you.

Please,
I need you
To let me back in.

Tess Pfeifer

First Love

We met each other in seventh grade at Van Sickle Junior High. That was the year I hated *Home Economics*, the year I no longer heard my teachers. I wanted *Shop*. It was right next door. Noises emanated from *Shop* that could make your blood course through your veins. My heart beat as the saws whirred and the hammers pounded. The voices that I could hear from the hallway were loud and full of excitement. You could smell that earth smell of wood.

In *Home Economics* we stirred our eggs and cooked them on a stove, made oatmeal, and cookies and did some sewing. I didn't know I was fortunate. I did these things at home and didn't want to do them at school. It seemed that real things were made in *Shop*—a table, a stool, something to store things in. In the girls' class (if you were in the box labeled "girl" you had to take *Home Economics* class) everything was gobbled up, leaving you with nothing. Empty-handed.

This was the year of Judgment and Humiliation. My first humiliation came early: The first English class. Did I know how to spell certain words? When the teacher said, "the" it sounded like a different species from anything I had ever heard. I wrote it after great trouble: *though*—no that's not how: *tha, thoug, thu*? I unraveled. Because of my shyness, I found myself word-dumb, unable to speak or think. And there, right on paper, was proof of my stupidity. I was stumped.

Where my teachers once had mouths, they now had holes. Nothing made sense. Except the science teacher. Miss Worthy (not her real name) wore long cotton dresses with a belt under her pancake-flat breasts. She told us—told me, a bath taker—that we mustn't take baths because we never really get clean if we wash in our own dirt. She would look at each of us as if we were filthy. I wanted her to see me and know, *not me, not me. I am not one of them, I'm clean!* But of course I was one of them; in 1967, I sat at the table with them, I listened with them, I saw her flat pancakes with them.

That was the year that I started wearing makeup after leaving the house. My lipstick was purple, a light, frosty purple that I'd found at a drug store beside Steiger's Department Store on Main Street. My best friend was a red-headed girl born on the same day as I was born. We said we would be best friends forever. And we swore everything about us was the same. I'll never forget her red hair.

How we spent our days, I don't recall except boys became the source of all our trouble. She started it. She spent more and more time with one boy. Then she wanted me to tag along. She made it her business to find a boy for me—Michael. Poor Michael.

One afternoon we slipped into the woods, beside the school parking lot. Michael made a tiny red star on my neck. I had noticed some girls wearing this bruise of adventure in the hallway. But I wasn't willing to put up a sign showing I was one of them. I was mad and kept silent. No one had ever made a mark on me. And kissing was more like having a railroad track slammed upside your mouth.

I felt ashamed. I took the bus home feeling that I wanted to break his neck.

That evening Michael called and said he loved me. I told him it wasn't that I didn't like him, I just didn't want to see him again, EVER. Then he started to cry. And then I hung up. I felt afraid and not ready for the things that were happening to me. I didn't know how to explain that to him. Hanging up was the only thing I could think of to do.

The next day I walked up to her, my best friend, on the front steps of the school as we were all piling into the building. I took a fistful of her hair and holding strong, I tore with all my might. I can still hear her scream and feel the school stop at her alarm. Time stood still, and I was left with a handful of red hair, the white roots writhing like shocked tendrils squirming for air.

Linda Keiderling

He Loves Me, Loves Me Not

"Hey Marley! What's up?" Sarah asked cheerfully.

"Oh, nothing much. I'm just going to wait here on the bleachers for Rick, he has practice today and really wanted me to be here."

"Okay, your choice, but there's a bunch of girls going to the mall . . . change your mind any???"

"I can't, I mean I promised Rick I would be here."

"Whoa, Marley! Let me get this straight, you would rather be watching a football practice than go to the mall with your best friend? Hmm, it just doesn't seem like you. I'll call you later, o.k.?"

Marley watched as the guys started to gather their gear and head to the field for the practice. She could see Rick, his helmet in hand and a nasty look on his face. Oh man, Marley thought, what did I do now?

Just as she thought, the practice was long and boring and she wished she had gone to the mall with the girls. Especially with Sarah, her best friend. She always had a great time with her.

The practice was over and Rick approached Marley with the same gnarly look on his face as earlier. She knew that look by now and started to tense up.

"You were five minutes late! You were not watching me the whole time, and I thought that I told you to never talk to that girl Sarah ever again." And with that he slammed Marley on the knee with his helmet. "What are you going to do, Marley, cry? You're such a child; I don't even know why I bother with you." And practically in the same sentence he apologized! Blaming his foul mood on a poor practice and having so much homework.

"Marley, I'm so sorry. Let me make this up to you, come on, I'll buy you your favorite milkshake." She thought, okay, he's under a lot of pressure and just needs to blow off some steam. As Marley stood up, her knee reminded her that that is not the right way to do it.

"Come on, Marley, don't make me wait if you want that milkshake. We have to go. Now!"

All Marley could think of was how she wished she had gone with Sarah and the other girls to the mall.

The milkshake was excellent as always; too bad she couldn't say the same about the conversation. "Hurry up, Marley, I have better things to do, than to keep drinking these milkshakes and you'll soon look like the cow that gave the milk!"

The waitress heard the snide remark that Rick had made and whispered to Marley, "He's not treating you right. You deserve better, Hun."

Somewhere in the back of Marley's mind, she knew the waitress was right. But she loved Rick. Not everyone is perfect; people say the wrong things sometimes, right? Not all relationships are perfect. There are bound to be bumps on the road ahead. Kind of like the one she now has on her knee. But he did say that he was sorry.

"That's it!" Rick said. "You're fat enough. Let's leave."

While outside the Dairy House, Rick asked what the waitress had said to her. But of course Marley wasn't going to tell him what the waitress said. "She said that I was with a very handsome young man." And with that said, Rick punched her in the stomach.

"You're a liar, you're fat and stupid! You don't deserve me, you don't even deserve the time of day from me, you're just a no good . . ." and as Rick's voice trailed off, Marley thought that the waitress was right. But what do I do? No one is going to believe that Rick is a bully and that he hits me! I feel so alone.

"Rick," Marley asked in a very nervous tone, "maybe we should take a break, ya know, not spend so much time together?"

"Oh really? How would you like it if I told Tonya about what you feel about her 'fashion style?' Or that you think Sarah's boyfriend is ugly?"

"No, no please, Rick. I'm sorry. I didn't know what I was thinking. I don't want to take a break in our relationship, I promise. I just thought that maybe with your football and all your homework that it would be easier on you if you didn't feel like you needed to make time for me."

And with that, came a punch to Marley's shoulder. "You're an idiot!" Rick grunted through clenched teeth, "Marley, I'm going home now and I will call you at six o'clock sharp. If you don't answer the phone, or if you're not there, I swear I don't know what I'll do to you."

"I'll be home, Rick. I'll be home studying alone. I promise." And just as she thought she was going to make her escape from anything else he had to say, "And remember, I said to stay away from that girl Sarah!"

As Marley limped her way back home, she thought, she really thought about how Rick had been treating her for the last year. He decides who she can and cannot talk to. What she can and cannot do in her spare time. And ugh! He tells her she's fat??? She's lost twenty pounds in the last six months! Marley thought that the bullying thing was bad, but now he's hitting her! Maybe I'm not always a good person and I still don't know what I've done, but I am afraid to ask him because I'm afraid that he'll hit me.

Sarah, I need Sarah. I can talk to her and she won't degrade me or abuse me.

And that's just what Marley did; she called Sarah even though Rick told her not to.

As a true friend Sarah came right away when Marley said that she needed to talk about something really important. Sarah arrived at five o'clock and she and Marley just sat in silence in Marley's bedroom. It may have even been hours before Sarah broke the silence.

"Marley?" Marley was startled when Sarah called her name.

"Yes, what is it?"

"I'm worried about you. You're acting strange."

"Sarah, can we please talk?"

I love Sarah, she's my best friend, but if I tell her, I just don't think that she will understand. He did say he would never do it again and I really want to believe him.

"Marley, please. It looks like you haven't slept in weeks, you've lost so much weight and you failed all your mid-term exams! Marley, I can see something is very wrong."

Sarah is right. I do need to talk to someone about it. Not that she is the only one who will understand and know what to do. But where do I start?

"Sarah, it's about Rick and our relationship."

"But you two have been together for almost three years and are most likely going to be crowned King and Queen at the prom! I can't imagine what could be wrong? Oh, Marley, is he cheating on you?"

Marley responded: "No, he's not and I'm not in love with him anymore. Actually, I'm afraid of him. I am so afraid of him."

"Marley, what do you mean you're afraid of him?"

As Marley's eyes began to fill with tears, she bowed her head and began to speak softly of the relationship that she has with Rick that no one else knew about but her. "People know Rick as a great football player, the most popular and most handsome guy in school. Rick is simply perfect. Too perfect, Sarah. He knew where to hit me so that people wouldn't see the bruises. He knew the perfect gift to give me when he apologized and swore that he would never do it again."

"Marley, when did this start happening?"

"About a year ago, but it's gotten so much worse. He calls me names; he's always telling me I'm stupid. He doesn't let me go anywhere that I want to go. Oh, Sarah, I lied to him and told him I was home studying, he doesn't even want me talking to you. I just don't know what to do, I'm so afraid."

She even told Sarah about every time he had hit her.

"Marley, the first thing we need to do is tell your parents and the school principal. If he's hitting and bullying you like this now, it could get so much worse! I read on the School Highlights Board that there is a group that meets once a week. It's for people who have been bullied, and I will go with you if you want. You can always count on me and your parents to be there for you. Always remember that you are not alone. I will even come with you to tell your parents about what Rick has been doing to you."

Gabriel Fontes

School

The sound was something along the lines of a growl. I was too tired to let the rage flow into a scream, and yet too restless to let this one go by.

"Hey!" I barked, tearing my hand from under his shoe.

Lucas towered above me, his blonde hair suspended just above his crooked smile. His foot was planted on the card that I was reaching for, that I rightfully deserved. The game was simple, whoever's card landed closest to the wall got to take all the cards thrown previously. There was no mistaking my victory, my throw actually landed on the crook of a brick, on the wall, inches closer than his. "I need those cards," I said, my voice cracking with resentment, "My last one is there."

He swept the cards into a pile, and pocketed them into his bag. All along encouraging snickers from onlookers. That's when I broke, my voice drained from wild hysterics to solemn moans.

I was still seated on the floor, oblivious to the puddle seeping into my pants. "Please . . . C'mon . . . What have I done to you?"

He didn't even shoot me a glance. Not only was he above speaking to me, but to bother looking at me would be a strain.

I was done. Why the hell bother, I thought. So I trudged down the stairs and resumed my lonesome spot in the bathroom stall.

Michael Amato

Little Brother

Bullies are monsters that exist outside of the closet and from under the bed; plus, they do not need darkness to make them even more of a menace. They are monsters that a person battles every day in the real world, which is the scariest thing about them—they live within our reality, making it a complete and utter nightmare. Nobody shares the horrifying tales of bullies around the campfire; instead people fabricate stories of vampires and ominous spirits from a parallel universe. It is bullies that loom in hallways of high school and spread rumors, creating an epidemic among students and giving its victims symptoms of nausea, nerves, and goosebumps that raise the hairs on the back of the neck.

Bullies come in all different shapes and sizes. They can be a dad, a policeman, a best friend—people that appear to be allies, confidants who turn into the worst fiends of all. As an alumnus of the geek click in high school, I battled my fair share of bullies who put glue in my seat, called me a faggot, and made me regret my very existence.

But the most horrifying bully tale that haunts me the most is about my little brother, a kid that walked in rhythm with his peers whose footsteps kept pace with his peer's treading the halls. Till one afternoon in March he fell out of stride with his class when he had a fight with the Hulk Hogan of his high school.

He stepped into a ring with a perimeter that grew the size of a football field. When the fight was over my brother was bruised and slightly concussed; however, there was no ringing of a bell to acknowledge the fight was over. Every hit was a click of a camera taking a photograph that developed into my brother's head. The stains of blood on a t-shirt were not enough to eternalize this image of self-defeat. Bleachers that were empty soon became filled as word spread re-creating the fight.

Soon the reel of film that was playing in my brother's head was being projected for his class to see. One spectator taped the fight and broadcasted it on the Internet. The wrestler won; the fight was another victory to his long list of wins on the mat. Hulk Hogan then used the footage to attest to his finesse and ability to overpower another and to further torment his opponent. His concept of the fight was to get my brother on the ground and beat the shit out of him till his dignity was shattered—his goal was achieved.

My brother has been struggling with apraxia his entire life, a disability that makes him vulnerable in social arenas such as high school. He is not able to verbally express himself. Mario is not a mute but he shuts down; he is unable to communicate. The fight showed him that he could not defend himself physically as well as verbally. His bullies always have an intangible, invisible hand placed upon his mouth, an imaginary leech sucking his confidence. His quiet, stealthy airs kept him from being noticed—it was his camouflage, which kept him from being targeted. Till the bright flamboyancy of a girl brought attention to him, bringing him under the bully's radar, a former friend.

It was not just any teenybopper; it was the wrestler's ex-girlfriend. A girl off limits to all, she was still a piece of his property whom he had yet to relinquish. The girl nestled in the arms of another hurt the credentials of this athlete, making him look inferior and the only way to reclaim his superiority was to take out the competition.

When a fight is over and the loser is on the ground the loser gains more enemies and more bullies because allegiances are formed with the winner. The video that was accessible on the Internet was being advertised in schools. Through flyers, e-mails, and word of mouth. But what halted the video from getting a huge number of hits was when the vice principal became aware of the situation and called the jock into his office. No punishment was given; just a warning to remove the video. This administrator feared the impact it could have on the boy's wrestling career.

There has always been nepotism in high school where the administration looks at jocks as their own children, their own pride and joy. They foster them for their agility and skill in order to receive praise in local articles and a trophy in a display case. The negligence of the school to discipline *boy wonder* caused more traumas because it allowed the kid in the letterman jacket to remain high and mighty. It furthered the inferiority of my brother, proving he was nothing to protect or acknowledge.

It is so easy when you're young to get rid of monsters because a parent can check under the bed, buy a night-light, and close the closet doors. However, when you're all grown up, parents are not able to get rid of these monsters that easily. My mother advocated for my brother on day one, never yielding in her pursuit to protect him. But the army of rogue warriors was growing to protect this kid in order to keep him on the wrestling mat. The vice principal played ignorant and the police claimed they were powerless. Instead of others helping to alleviate the mental pain of my brother and disciplining the boy, they were trying to make sure the kid could still roll around in his unitard pinning another boy to the ground. The police advocated for *Joe athlete* because one of the policemen on the force coached him and valued him. They were sweeping the incident under the rug, creating a mountain to grow underneath the carpet.

Since the fight, Mario has been battling post-traumatic stress disorder. The fight was more than water cooler gossip at school; it was a gasser that spouted out many stories. It brought Mario face to face with more rumors that kept him on the ground at the park. He never really had gotten up; he is still lying there. He did not feel safe; he was exposed as a weak person. His peers acting like tabloids sending out text messages about his love life, hooking him up with girls that were already linked to people made him an object of prey for more guys to hunt. He was getting bad publicity and he did not have a press agent; he could not speak for himself and he had no one to speak on his behalf. Mario was the pinball that was being hit through the hallways, peers earning points making bells and whistles go off when they got a reaction that jostled him. The fight catapulted him into a foreign world, where he was a game to play, a temper to accelerate. He was drowning in the lies and speculation kept him below a shield of Plexiglas; he could no longer breathe.

He wanted to leave high school, his home—everything. He saw nothing but grey and a rainy forecast. The torrential gossip soaked him and chilled him, making him long for warmth. Mario wanted to kill himself. He wrote a note addressing his family and friends of his decision, concluding it with: "Peace out, West Side." Fortunately, my mother found his note before he was able to commit any fatal act. He was admitted into the hospital and underwent therapy and psychiatric help to dispel the curses of worthlessness his peers led him to believe. It was like a preservation, which took in injured teens with broken spirits and cast them in a sense of self-security before releasing them back into their wild habitats.

Even with his new sense of self and knowledge gained through therapy, my brother is still angry. He is still mad at the monsters that haunt him and hurt him. He has not been able to let go of the horror he faced, but holds onto it. Since this quarrel he cracks if a CD skips or if a DVD has a glitch. These small incidents bring him back to the ground where he laid on that afternoon in March. The memories are cancerous and spread rage through the body, leaving a craving in his stomach that hungers for revenge, justice, something he knows that will not be granted to him.

Monsters never disappear even when you get older. There will be one as a boss, as a politician, and even as an in-law. But the key is overcoming them, which my brother is still struggling with. The incident controls his life because no justice was granted to him. He cannot come to terms with the fight; it is his nightmare and his reality. Vampires, witches, goblins, and werewolves are nothing compared to corrupt policemen, jocks, ignorant principals, and catty peers. These are the bullies that create real horror stories because they are the faces you sometimes never outgrow and never get past.

John Kuebler

Dirge for Eliezer

He was bigheaded,
a bucktoothed booger eater,
made to wear his yarmulke to school.

Certainly no top tier type
nor alpha male, me, I
still had face to save—
still had to assert my standing:
one

above
him.

Secretly we met
for chess matches on doorsteps,
or Holmes Park I remember one time
at dusk, batting and shagging balls.
I was after his mind and
he was in need of my body.

Which is how I happened
to be there after school when
the bunch of biggest
bad asses jumped him.
I did not lend him my fists
as our loose-fitted allegiance
called for, for treachery was
the easier road.

He kept his feet and bore
my laughter with resolve,
as if he understood how
difficult it must be for me,
holding up without a spine.

Diane Lefer

A Two-Minute Play

Setting: A 4th-grade classroom.

Characters:
The TEACHER
BECKY, nine-year-old girl

TEACHER: Who has a story to tell? (BECKY waves her hand, volunteering.) Becky? (The TEACHER sits and Becky stands in front of the class.)

BECKY: OK, this girl was walking home from school and a boy came up behind her. She turned around because he was whispering something but she couldn't hear. He made an ugly face at her so she kept walking, faster. But she could hear him walking faster behind her. She could hear him breathing. And then she started to hear his words: You think you're so smart! Someone's gonna teach you a lesson. Well, she was smart. Everyone in school knew that, and she did not want any lesson a boy like that could teach. So she walked faster. So did he.

He said, 'Tomorrow I'll be carrying a fishing rod. It will have a big, sharp hook at the end of the fishing line. I'm going to throw it so it hooks your back. Then I'm going to pull it, so it tears your skin. Then I'm going to hook it deeper so it tears your flesh.'

She was so scared. She wanted to run but she didn't want him to see how scared she was. He was bigger and taller and could probably run faster. Just two more blocks till she got home.

'I have a knife in my pocket,' he said. 'I wonder what it will look like in your back!'

The girl screamed. And she ran. And guess what? It's a true story. The boy was Bobby and the girl was me!

TEACHER: Becky! Enough! See me in the hall. (TEACHER and BECKY move to "the hall.")

I know you think you did the right thing, but Bobby's a very sensitive boy. You've just embarrassed him in front of everyone.

BECKY: But he—

TEACHER: You're smart enough to know better. You should have spoken to me in private.

BECKY: What about what he did—?

TEACHER: He probably followed you and said those things just because he likes you. That's how boys show they like a girl.

BECKY: Ew! Maybe I don't want anyone to like me! Is that really—?

TEACHER: Just think about other people's feelings next time.

THE TEACHER puts a friendly arm around BECKY, gives her a pat, and then exits.

BECKY: What about my feelings?

CURTAIN.

Suni Paz

Alias, "La Nata"

"La Nata? What kind of name is that?" Grandmother asked me.

It was her nature to scrutinize my friends' last names to screen me from any influence that lacked an upstanding lineage. I was to dismiss any friends from my life whose family lacked the required social status. In this category stood La Nata, but he wasn't even my friend; he was my enemy.

His countenance was wild for his red hair flew straight out from his head and fell about his face whichever way the wind blew, covering at times his two small eyes. La Nata was lean, quick as a hare, and mean-spirited. In my view, his cowardice prevailed over all of his other characteristics. He consistently went after the youngest, smallest, and most defenseless children. Even at nine years old, I had no tolerance for bullies. I couldn't stand them and I especially couldn't bear La Nata. I decided to keep a close eye on him and wait for the right moment. Then I would make him pay for all the miseries he had bestowed on others.

La Nata could see that I was observing him. In response, he began staring at me, teasing and making off-color and inane jokes, showing off his skills at jumping rope and running. He was definitely trying to impress me. At recess, his loud and belligerent voice overshadowed all others as he tore around the schoolyard, throwing balls at girls' legs, pulling hair, and bothering everyone.

Like a spider, I waited patiently for my day to come.

Monday arrived. It was so cold we wore our coats in class. At recess, to adjust to a teacher's absence, we were told to change classes and we left the classroom carrying our school bags, heavy with books.

On the patio, we encountered a great commotion. La Nata had cornered my small friend Julie and was throwing eucalyptus cones at her legs. Julie commenced crying, helplessly, while La Nata's friends stood by laughing at her. Her cricket-like jumps in self-defense were useless, for La Nata aimed with cruel accuracy.

Coming upon this scene, I couldn't help but see red. Without thinking, I ran towards La Nata and with all my might rammed his right shoulder with my own. We both lost our balance, but before he had regained it, I pounded his back with my bag full of books. Taken by surprise, he appeared to become so dizzy that he collapsed full length on the ground. I hit him yet again for the third time and for good measure collected the cones he had thrown, and one by one, I threw them at him. Then, imitating my brothers, I stood up tall and shouted for everyone to hear:

"Rotten little coward, if I see you bothering any girl here or in class, or harming any child, you are dead. We'll all get you. Do you hear? We'll all get you!"

The kids in the schoolyard liked the fact that I had included them in the threat and roared in approval.

The truth was that, but a few friends, who probably feared him more than liked him, nobody really approved of his bullying. He happened to be the oldest kid in our school, held over due to his grades.

It was neither the words nor the blows but the public humiliation that stopped La Nata. His friends gloried in recounting in great detail the story of his fall. As the days went by, the story grew more outrageous. As the tale evolved, La Nata appeared to be a villain while my friends were revered as valiant heroes. I was no longer part of the picture.

As the oldest student in our school, La Nata had never been confronted before and no limits had ever been put on his actions. As I was the first one to do just that, he fell in love with me, totally. He was a thirteen year old smashed by first love.

We first noticed his change several days later when La Nata came to school with his hair combed. The relentless teasing his little effort at etiquette drew, he was able to fix with a few well-placed blows. Shortly thereafter he began to do good deeds here and there. Amazed, we took care not to say a single word. La Nata began offering the girls the one and only seat in the playground, which, until then, had been his throne. He could be seen helping the smallest children swing, and everyone else with their books and bags. He had become almost completely unrecognizable.

While his good deeds were taking place, La Nata would glance over at me, hoping to be noticed. Notice I did, but not a word or a smile came out of me. I was going to let him taste his medicine to the hilt. Now I had become really mean. La Nata began writing notes. The first, complete with spelling errors, apologized for having chosen my friend Julie as the target of his cones. As the letter showed no remorse for throwing the cones, only for the choice of victim, I was infuriated. The second note spoke of his desire to be my friend. In the third one he offered to carry my bag and to share his lunch with me. Finally, he got up the courage and confessed his love.

Meanwhile, in school, everyone made fun of him behind his back. His puppy love was the subject of endless joking and the whole school seemed to know that it was not reciprocal. I began to feel sorry for him. Feigning innocent eyes and in a singsong voice my classmates would chant:

"Was it Love with a big L or just the whack with the bag that changed him? No!!! The books helped to enlighten his hard head! It seems the only way he'll learn is through books—so whack him again!"

Making him the butt of such jokes was infectious but I could see that it had gotten out of hand. Sensing his humiliation, I began to commiserate with him. Hoping to spare him further ordeal, I started talking to La Nata as if nothing had ever happened between us. In time, my friends too began accepting him like one of the crowd.

La Nata and I never really became friends, in part, because his tendency to follow me around like a hound, with sorrowful eyes, remained off-putting. But our dealings with each other from then on were civilized and he was no longer the center of cruel jokes. From La Nata, I learned that a combination of bitter and sweet, judiciously applied, could soften a person's character and bring out the best in him.

Soon after, La Nata's family moved and we never heard or saw him again. There are moments in which I wonder what became of him, for La Nata was the first boy that loved me blindly and told me so, although I was not ready for such devotion. I picture his red, unruly hair that gave his beseeching face the appearance of having been touched upon by a dark wind.

Angela Kariotis

BULLIEZ

Don't tell anybody. Sometimes I act like I'm sick even when I'm really not, so I can stay home from school that day. No big secret. But especially Tuesdays and Thursdays, which also happen to be gym days. I like the games, but it gets so loud with big bursting echoes in the gym, slipping and sliding on wood floors. I can play, but I'm not fast and can't throw hard for dodge ball, and everybody makes fun of me. But I don't see why you have to be so fast or throw that hard; it's still playing. I get picked almost last. Especially when Laura and Sandy, the popular girls, are the captains. Laura doesn't need to say to Sandy, "Ooh, pick me, pick me! Yeah! Okay, okay, don't pick her; she's awful." It's understood. Another girl, Jane, gets picked last a lot. I'm not all that good, I guess, but she's worse, if you can believe it. What makes somebody get picked first anyway?

Even with so many kids running like crazy all around, it's extra lonely that way.

What do Policemen do?
What do Butterflies do?
What do BULLIES do?
BULLIES!?
They
Punch   kick   mean   copy   hurt   take   push   laugh

bullies kick hurt take laugh
at who?
bullies laugh at not with
bullies make-fun of,
      making fun of someone makes sadness for the kid you're making
      fun of
that's no fun
bullies laugh at me and you
bullies use words that hurt

you're a shorty | that's ugly| eww | you look like a boy| what's the
   matter with you, got a problem?| no you can't play with us | you're a
   cry baby| stupid| Joel Joel Jelly-Roll Joel Joel Jelly-Roll| ha ha ha|
bullies write down their words instead of saying them, but we can still
   hear the hurt
"Psst, Laura, take this note!" | Jane is really fat and ugly and I don't want
   her to sit next to me in art class. I hate her. She is a loser with no
   friends. No one sit next to her, okay? Circle okay and pass this note
   on. | Okay. Psst . . .

bullies use their bodies to cause hurt
give me that, you can't have it| get away |
punch | kick | push | shove |
you want these back, come and get'em four-eyes|
bullies laugh at me and you
At
lunch| in class| at recess| at gym| on the bus| when the teacher isn't
   looking| after-school!

Lunch is not like sitting in class because in class you have your desk.
It's the same desk all the time, but at lunch you sit wherever so it can be
some place different every day. Sandy tells everybody where to sit, or Laura
does. Only Laura and Sandy always sit next to each other. I don't know
who made them boss, but everybody listens like they have to. Laura says,
"Okay, you sit here because I'm sitting here, and you sit there because I'm
sitting here." Laura and Sandy, I mean, could be so mean! Like they try to
make everybody else who's not them sad with just the things they say or
do. Laura makes fun of my hair, "Your mom put a bowl on your head and
cut all around it!" I hate my hair so much I just want to chop it off, but it's
so short already. That's why she makes fun of it, or I wear a hat. I like to
wear hats. The truth is I don't hate my hair. I hate that Laura hates my hair,
and I wish she wouldn't. No matter how mean she is, though, I'd still like
Laura to be my friend. I mean too that I can be her friend. I am her friend.

How do BULLIES make us feel?
I feel
Hurt| sad| scared to go to school everyday| alone|

Maybe we say in our head,
> Telling a bully, "You can't do things like that!" is easy to say when you are someone else.

Maybe we think,
> No matter where you are there will always be people who'll make fun of you.

Maybe we feel,
> Why me? Not again!

She broke my lunchbox! He ripped my coat!

She smooshed my glasses!

She says nasty things about me! He hits me on the back really hard at gym!

They made fun of the clothes I wear! They made fun of the color of my skin!

They said I was dirty! They made fun of my mom! They laughed at my crutches!

You can't do things like that!

I just want to be friends. I feel scared to go to school every day.

Standing up to a bully is hard, so we say in our head,
> Maybe it will go away.
> What did I do wrong?
> Why me? Not again!

No, it's not your fault! Say: "It's not my fault!" We didn't do anything wrong!

It's all girls in the class mostly. And it switches whose turn it is to get picked on, but it's never Sandy or Laura's turn ever. They start it. And it's up to them to decide when they don't feel like being mad at you anymore. So they turn it off and on just like that for no reason either way, just depends on what they feel like, I guess. I didn't want it to be my turn but with only 15 kids in the class it's gonna be my sad turn eventually, so they'd laugh or talk about me, but mostly just not let me do what they would be doing, nothing fun, no laughing with them. I know what it feels like so I would not make anybody else feel like that too, but when it came to someone else's turn to get picked on I was just glad it wasn't me anymore. I joined in doing what I knew didn't make somebody feel very good. It was Jane's turn a lot. Laura says, "If you want to be our friend since we're popular you can't be Jane's friend, okay?" I was always Jane's friend, but I said, "Okay." I didn't mean to make Jane sad, it's just that everybody else was doing it, and I was scared to say, Stop, you can't do things like that! But then it became my turn to get picked on again (so Laura and Sandy were just my fake friends). Jane didn't do anything mean to me, even when I was mean to her because I felt like I had to. I was never mean again to anybody. I don't care who is my friend or not. You can't do things like that. When someone hurts your feelings, you feel like an outsider not an insider. I know what that feels like, and I don't want to make someone feel that way.

What do we do when we are BULLIED?
Bullies think they scare everybody but when you stand up to a bully they get scared.
You can't fight back because that's not the answer, but you can talk to them. You have to tell someone.
You have to tell someone else like a teacher or your mom or dad, or another grown-up because they can help. And it's okay to tell them because everybody knows what it feels like because teachers and moms and all grown-ups were kids once too, just like you.
A bully can make you feel lonely but you are not alone. It doesn't have to be like this. It's like math homework; there are answers to every problem. Being bullied is a problem that can be solved. Together.

Going home is the best since I won't be at school anymore. I climb up the stairs to my room and I feel safe. I like everything in my room and everything in my room likes me. My mom saw that I was sad today so she asked what was wrong. I told her one of the boys from school was making fun of my name. After school is bad too 'cause there are no teachers around. My mom asked me what he said. "He called me Ang-Jelly Sandwich!" "Well that doesn't sound so bad. You shouldn't get so upset over that, come on now." But it did make me so upset. I don't even know why. Maybe it was because he was huddled around all the other boys and he's screaming out Ang-Jelly Sandwich when he sees me waiting to go home. Or maybe it was the way he laughed. It wasn't just what he was saying, but why he was saying it, and the way, everything, it's not just the words. I explained it to my mom and she said, "Everything is going to be okay. Thank you for telling me this. You know you can come to me about anything and I will help you. It's not your fault." And she took me to school the next day and talked to my teacher. My teacher was very nice, I like him; he's a good teacher. He said, "It's not your fault. We can solve this problem together. You are not the only one who feels like this. Other kids are being bullied too and want it stop like you do. I'm glad you told your mom because now we know what's going on and we can stop it." I was not alone. I felt happier about being in school and safe, like I feel when I am in my room.

Who are BULLIES?
Bullies are KIDS too!
Bullies are mean and hurt your feelings.
Bullies pick on smart kids and call them dorks.
Bullies want to copy off of them.
Bullies make fun of everybody else and don't stop until they make
     you cry.
Maybe bullies are the way they are because someone bullied them, so now
     they want to get back at somebody.
But a bully can be a nice person too once you get to know them.
Bullies are KIDS too!
Bullies are sometimes your classmates and your best friends.
Bullies aren't always mean.
Maybe bullies wouldn't be bullies if they got some extra love and
     attention.
Maybe their parents can help them to stop being bullies by helping them
     do their homework.
Or knowing it is okay to ask for help with anything when they need it.
We have to help bullies stop being bullies.
We have to help bullies not want to be bullies.
I don't mean to be mean.
Why do bullies want to be mean?
Bullies, don't you know it's better to be a friend than a bully?
Being a bully is lonely too.
Laughing at someone is making-fun by yourself and that's sad.
But laughing with them is making-fun together!
Don't have sad!
Have fun!

Stop in the track,
Throw mud on back.
Stop that leave me!
Force smack push hit
Hey give me that!
Think smart not mean.
Sad mad hurt cry
Pain blame feels real
Stop turn run hide
Sue Tom Bob Jill
Wound sore bruise heal.

Puma Perl

Girls

the girls had a secret.

they cupped pink
hands around rosebuds
razor blades glinted
from the corners
of their eyes.

i felt their sharp giggles
cutting into my ribs.

lunch was over
and we waited
for our counselor
by the basement steps.

Swimming was next.
it was the best
part of day camp.
nobody bothered you
and you didn't look
funny under water.

the girls knotted together,
whispering and laughing.

we'll tell you the secret,
they said,
when we get to the fifth floor.

suddenly, i knew.
i'd left my little bag
in the cafeteria

"my purse!" i shouted,
like a lost old lady,
desperately searching
for her battered
plastic handbag.

neither fat nor skinny,
nor pretty enough,
i ran back
to the lunchroom,
found the bag,
belongings intact:
bathing suit, cap,
my favorite book.

the girls were disappointed.
i had ruined their fun.
maybe they had enjoyed
the image of me
sitting miserably on the tiles,
swimsuit and Nancy Drew
lost forever in the cafeteria.

one of the girls was my friend.

they were mean
for the rest of the day,
but by the next morning
i was forgotten
and all that was left
was another day
spent alone,
waiting to swim.

Yolanda Maria-Rose Scavron

SNAP

She sat staring at her hands in her lap. If she was quiet enough maybe they wouldn't notice her today. Eyes squeezed shut. She willed herself to disappear. No such luck.

SNAP *SNAP* Tasha's bubble gum popped to her right.

They'd found her. She could hear Fi's pen tapping against the table to her left. Same routine every day. Well, it never hurt to hope. Even if it proved pointless.

SNAP *SNAP* The Lesson was about to begin.

Reaching to the right to grab a pen out her bag, she sits back up quickly. Tasha was to her right, Maybe, just maybe if the bag had been on Fi's side she'd have a chance, but Tasha was always looking for a fight. It could wait. Or maybe she could just borrow Melanie's notes later. She could never understand it. Out of all the seats in every class. Tasha and Fi always chose to sit, one on her left and one on her right. Trapping her. She was scared. Every time, but what could she say? Neither Tasha nor Fi had ever really threatened her. Neither had ever harmed her or even said anything mean to her. It was hard to explain. She had tried once, to tell her mom. Mom had said "Maybe the girls just want to be your friends." They didn't want to be her friend. She could tell. She could feel it.

Staring at her hands, she realized she couldn't hear Fi's pen tapping anymore. That was always the signal that the teacher had arrived to the room. Lessons were beginning. She couldn't look around. Just up and straight ahead. She didn't want Fi or Tasha getting any ideas that she was giving them the "eye." Sahara had given Tasha the eye once. Sahara had to switch schools.

SNAP *SNAP*
At least it was the last class of the day.
SNAP *SNAP*
Now all she had to survive was the bus ride.

Ronald Coolbeth

A Story about Bullying

My story begins when I started school at six years old. We lived in Lyndonville, Vermont. So six was the age children started grade school in the 1930s. I was a shy kid and was slow of speech and quite small for my age. I was the perfect target for bullies on and off the playground; I was picked on a lot. While I was walking home from school, kids would jump out from a hiding place and terrorize me.

I finally reached a breaking point and learned how to box. Then I started to fight back. It was at that point that my life changed. The bullies stopped picking on me. In fact, they wanted to be my friends. I wasn't bothered again after that.

My family moved around quite a bit. This meant changing schools often. I needed to prove myself at every new school, which, after learning how to box, wasn't a problem for me anymore.

Later, at the age of 14, I boxed in the Golden Gloves. I never had trouble with anyone again.

Now, I am 77 years old and still in good condition.

Well, for what it's worth, this is my story.

IDENTITY

"An identity would seem to be arrived at by the way in which the person faces and uses his experience."

—James Baldwin

Eilish Thompson

"Normal Girl Drama"

Written in response to an article circulating about Phoebe Prince's death resulting from bullying.

Let us shine this tragedy in a more positive light.
Because after all, kids will be kids,
And violence is normal.
Why wouldn't it be?
My 4 year old boasts
That he can shoot a gun
Better than his grandfather
Who fought in World War II,
Thanks to all those video games
I've bought him, instead of wasteful family vacations.
And my 16 year old daughter,
She knows more profane words and slurs
Than Webster,
And "name-calls" like a pro;
She's had years of practice
And observations at perfecting the fine art of
Teasing; childhood's inside jokes
Come naturally to her, as does popularity—
I must say though, and not to toot my own polished horn,
But the 150 dollar jeans I bought for her
Have really done her miracles.
As have her personal trainer, dietician, nutritionist, and plastic surgeon
    since age 13.
It's just simply never too early to start being perfect!
You see, she was gaining a bit of weight—
90 pounds at age 12! By God, and only 5 foot 5.
A bit large-chested; particularly in the heart area—
If I had to choose which area was the most affected
By those slumber parties and best friends of hers.
(makes disgusted face) Their breath always reeked of Cheetohs,

Mixed with their displays of sheer and utter happiness,
And tied together with a nice little bond of friendship
With "BFFE" written all over it, her room constantly stunk like
     unconditional love . . .
Ever tried to get that type of stain out of your 10,000 dollar carpet?
It's not easy.
But when necessity calls, mother has to answer.
Because mother knows best.
And anyone who disagrees
Can be expecting a flock of my pretties
To attack their self-esteem
Faster than you can come up with one reason
Why I should be punished
For teaching my children, and their (makes a face) "partners" in detecting
The slackers,
The sluts who steal any of their ex-boyfriends (they can share within the
     circle of course),
The ugly people,
The weirdos,
The disabled,
The weak majority,
And anyone else who just doesn't fit in with normal people,
And for making such . . . people see themselves the way
The Man (points skyward)
Intended for them to be seen:
Like they are creatures from Hell, deformed and damaged.

After all, that's life. It's life.
This is how children behave.
And it's all good . . .
Unless it's bad.
And then it just sucks for you.

Got a problem with me
Or my ways?
Write about it as some sort of comment
To an article that I can smell brewing in the near future.

Just get it all out
Online.

I hope you will continue to attack the ones-
My pretties—
Who will, and I can assure you of this-
Be the ones always
Blaming
The poor
Victim—
They are so good at distracting any and all efforts
That could have formed to try to destabilize this insanity.
(Laughs insanely)

Online—
That's where it is all born,
All crescendos like the finale of a requiem written by Satan himself
    (smiles at the thought)
And then dies.
Drops dead of its own accord.

Let it be known, as is proof,
That any attempt to "make us all just get along"
Will be blocked by your own failed and effortless efforts
At stopping this empire of hatred
I am building with your passive permission;
Your mediocre efforts
Have been deflated with a simple poke of my perfect, manicured and
    plastic nails;
They are the necks that I have broken by stepping all over.

So try to stop me,
Make your feeble attempts to catch me,
But—rest assured—
Or perhaps, more accurately—
Restlessly rest your head in feigned ignorance,
And continue to

Ignore the cry you hear at night- and perhaps have been hearing all too
    often in the girl's bathroom as of the beginning of the year—
Banish the look of hopelessness in the
Poor victim's eyes
To the back of her thoughts,
Until that hopelessness eats her subconscious sanity completely,
And devours the loser's desire to live.

And be assured
That my perfume
Will always
Mask my lack of substance,
Of love, and of friendship.
Because those things simply aren't for me or my pretties,
But for the weirdos and the weak.

Mirtha Quiroz

Solitude

In my first cry
In the air that I breathe
In a whisper
In a blink
In desire

In the chalk that I used
To draw on the doors
Of my closet;
In the frame without pages;
In the pencil I couldn't find.

En el regaño de mi madre
En la risa de la gente.
In my paintings
In my mind
In my body, in my memories

She was always there.

En la ropa que no podía comprar,
En los zapatos que deseaba tener

Ahí estába ella.

En mi boca
In the kiss that you gave me
In the essence of your body.

She was always there.

In the joy—in sickness
In the darkness—in clarity
As much in truth, as in a lie.

She was always there

There she remains faithful,
Faithful like a memory
Like time—like the cry
Like the dream
She is
Señora Soledad.

Eilianie M. Alvelo

To My Two Little Nephews

Writing is the way I try to see the world through your eyes.

Mamita and Daddy, I know you were eagerly expecting me and when I arrived, I seemed to be 'normal' in every way. I am sorry that it's been years and I still don't know how to call you 'mommy' and 'daddy,' I don't look at you in the eye, I don't want you kissing or hugging me and I don't get excited with my own birthday celebration. It's not that I don't love you. 'I love you' is what I want to say every night before I finally close my eyes. It's just hard for me to show you how I feel, how I think, how I perceive the world where I feel I don't belong to. I walk on my tiptoes and use toys in strange ways. My memory is filled up with pictures. My days are made up of pictures and it's tough for me to convert whatever you try to tell me because like I have learned: talking is not a picture. It is not something I can observe and witness in detail like I do with the tears coming down your face since the day we went to that doctor. My playing is based on patterns that unstoppably come to my mind. Patterns of colors, toys and pictures created by me . . . The great composer. Mami, my underwear bothers me in an unexplainable way. I don't like how these pieces of clothes rub against my skin. I can't stand when the environment is too loud and it's because of my senses! Don't you feel it?! Don't you hear it?! Didn't you see it?! This world bothers me! This is what gets me to spin, cry and run to my world to create patterns and to be what I was born to be: a victim of this spectrum. When I cry, I hurt myself. Not noticing that I'm doing so, but, I know I do. Most people think that my behavior and repetitive movements are odd. And indeed they are. But, for some reason I get comfort from it. I get calm . . . I get to be me; an autistic child.

Jha'nai Richardson

To Tell You the Truth

To tell you the truth,
I am labeled a bully,
A bully because I tease
people about their flaws.
I push people around,
when I know they are too weak
to fight back.
To tell you the truth,
I do these things because
when I was younger than I am now
people teased me because
I weighed more than many others.
To tell you the truth,
I was a victim of bullying.

Janis Astor del Valle

Trans Plantations

(Pre-show music fades out. Stage is dark. Spotlight comes up center stage on MI, Puerto Rican woman, early 40's, lying on the floor, clad in a strait-jacket and pajamas, as she awakens. The effect is that of a specimen in a jar.)

MI: I'm so tired . . . I'm so tired . . . I am so tired. I don't remember the exact moment I got IN—it's all a blur . . . one moment I was chopping sofrito for my girlfriend's omelette—one moment I was loving her, one moment I was loving my Self, and the next, I was OUT . . . I was OUT, but not really OUT . . . I mean I was OUT, like a light . . . OUT like a light on the deconstructed Bruckner Expressway . . .

(She notices her leg. Full lights come up slowly as she straightens up, rising. We see four chairs toppled over, strewn about the stage.)

Mami
Taught Me
Not to shave
"If God had wanted us to shave, he would've made us bald!"
She . . .
The vivacious cadence of her alto voice makes everyone stop
To look.

Puerto Rican womanhood donning the body of a German kommandant;
Shoulders flung back in exuberant pride,
Thick, strong arms
Coupled with long, slender hands that refuse to salute,
Eyes and chin tilted ever so skyward,
Heart and bosom up and out—
Is she really only five-foot-six?

I thrived, my first seven years in the Bronx. And though I spent the next 15 transplanting my little Puerto Rican self into rural Connecticut, I've always considered myself a city kid at heart. Those early days, mami and me buying plátanos and ajo at Hunts Point – it used to smell so good then, as pure and gentle and strong as mami's kitchen – Christmas shopping at Alexander's in Parkchester or Korvette's on White Plains Road, meeting Papi for real pizza on Westchester Square, bein' babysat by my big brother Linky who got me hooked on the 4:30 movie and Frank Sinatra and Humphrey Bogart and Edward G. Robinson and James Cagney, "rat-a-tat-tat, you dirty rat" . . . those early days, vibrant colors and thunderous rhythms, keep my heart beating and my head reeling . . . I don't remember the exact moment I got IN—it's all a blur . . . one moment I was chopping sofrito for my girlfriend's omelette and the next, I was OUT . . . I was OUT, but not really OUT . . . I mean, I was OUT, like a light . . . OUT like a light on the deconstructed Bruckner Expressway . . . and then I woke up, and suddenly found myself strapped IN . . . but, it wasn't sudden at all . . . this was 40 years in the making . . . (On knees, struggling to remove straitjacket.)

Childhood was
hanging on catch
phrases like a fish out of water—

¡No digo yo!
¡Poca vergüenza!
¡Pal' carajo,
Coño!
Estás borracho—

(standing) mami and papi
start speaking
Perfect English when they think
i'm listening
but I want to hear more
catch phrases thrown
around our New England

house like my brother's handball
on our old schoolyard wall
to wall
P.S. 93

oh, say can you see me
here, beneath the corn
stalks, I'm trying to get off
this farm but these weeds
are too high
(jumping onto cube) we used to live in the Bronx, in a hi-rise,
fifth floor, 5-A, 955
Evergreen and Story Av
we had a terrace and I could wave
to Maria, Joaquin and Eddie D
I used to see my people for miles
oye, can you hear me?
I'm comin' down!
(jumps off cube) can't see nothin' now
but land and noisy quiet
ain't no stickball
no amarillos
no coquito
no rice and beans
only in my mami's kitchen
once a week
'cause "IGA don't have no
Spanish food," mami says
we have to stock up
on our monthly trip
to the Bronx
to my tita's kitchen
in my Puerto Rican dreams . . .

(She crosses to CS, lifts up a chair with her foot and sits.)

1970 . . . I was in the middle of second grade when we left the Bronx—
population infinity. We moved to New Milford, Connecticut—population
five. Suddenly, we were the only Puerto Ricans for miles. 20/20 voted it
the typical New England town back in the 80's. "Poor, little New Milford!"
my mother would sing from time to time—and I never understood what
she found so poor about a town that was run by bankers and clergymen—

"Poor, little New Milford," she would almost chant, while washing dishes, or shoveling a path through six foot snow drifts. Three days after moving to Connecticut, Mami planned our first trip back to the Bronx, to Co-op City, to my Tito's—that's what we called my grandfather, Mami's father. It was New Year's Eve and Tito's birthday. Mami had made a gigantic pot of arroz con gandules—his favorite. We had two blizzards in as many days, totaling five and a half feet, plus drifts. Todavía, Mami was determined. We were going to New York, come hell or high water. Mami dispatched the troops to clear out the snow: She and my father on the driveway, me and my brother Jeff at the car. But, instead of a driveway, Mami and Papi uncovered a one-hundred foot sheet of ice. Mami wasn't singing "Poor little New Milford" this time. In fact, she wasn't singin', punto. (imitating Mami) She was only chopping, chopping away at that ice as if it were a garden of wayward garlic. Boy, could that woman chop ice—almost as fast as she chopped sofrito. Thirty-seven minutes later, we were all ready to pile in our '62 Rambler—(imitating) except Papi, who was carefully descending the outside stairs carrying, like the Holy Grail, the huge glass bowl of arroz con gandules. Suddenly, he slips, he slides, a thunderous thump, a thud of flesh against wrought iron and concrete, and the whir of the arroz con gandules zooming from my father's hands like a flying saucer, crashing and cracking into a heap of Papi, arroz, gandules and glass on ice. My father lay dazed at the foot of the stairs. And the first words out of Mami's mouth were: "AY, DIOS MIO, MY GANDULES!"

(working out of jacket) Feisty spirit of enlightenment carried out,
Up and over the trenches
Of a Sexist society
By an Olympic runner's hairy legs;

yet, she disdains
Movements.

(poking hand out of jacket) Her fears tiptoe extra slowly around what she
    perceives to be land
Mines, and she sometimes retreats:
(pulling hand back in) "I shave for special occasions—weddings
And funerals!"

Her husband didn't want her to work outside the home,
So she waited twenty-two years before taking a part-time position
At the local department store—

But her cheers quickly paved the way to my front line:
"Nena, don't EVER let a man
Make mincemeat out of you!"

She gives advice, I take commands. (MI salutes.)

Governed by tradition,
Half teasing, half jealous,
She labels me,
"Daddy's girl."
"No!" I insist, I love and respect my father, but he will always
Have the home team advantage—I am
My Mother's daughter.
Still, she doesn't want to believe
That she could be my hero; in her world,
Heroes are men
And women are women
(placing a leg on chair) Shaving and not shaving and not speaking Spanish
And still.
Still
Fighting losing battles.

My paradoxical hero,
My Mami.

(Imitating Papi shaving.)

How I loved shaving with papi . . . he was so handsome, and so beauti-
fully-groomed. Every Sunday morning, he'd let me stand beside him at the
bathroom sink.

At first, I would stare, fascinated by his
Meticulous, slow, precise

Gentle, big hands
Ever elegant in the embrace of his razor

And he'd trim his mustache with the big scissors—how did he do it, so steady? (begins her own shaving) Then, I'd follow, with the toy electric razor he'd bought me. The first time Mami saw us:

MAMI: Ay, que linda!

MI: But after six weeks of this precious ritual . . .

MAMI: Ay, ya! Cuca, c'mon, you have to try on the dress I bought you for Cousin Pepa's wedding!

(MI begins stomping in protest. Tito Puente and Eddie Palmieri's *El Bochinche* plays; the stomping turns into dancing as she sheds the straitjacket.)

MI: How is it that at all the Puerto Rican weddings I've been to, the women were always dancing—with each other—I mean, they would carry on! And nobody ever said nothin'. In fact, the men cheered them on! Mami was one of those women; when she got on the floor with her sistas, you couldn't stop them . . . kneeling at jacket) yet Mami, who fled the Jehovah's Witnesses because they were too restrictive, tells me homosexuality is a sin . . . (to audience) am I my mother's daughter?

(Lights change. She sets up two rows of chairs.)

MI: I was five the first time I went to Puerto Rico. Mami and me were visiting her family on the southern part of the island. We flew on a jumbo jet to San Juan, then switched to a rickety commuter plane for Ponce. Man, that thing looked like a leftover from the Wright Brothers. When its single engine started, I felt my whole body begin to shake. I thought it was nerves until I saw everybody else in the plane shakin', too. I had two handfuls of Hershey's Kisses—I squeezed them into fists, shut my eyes, echoed Mami's "Ay, Dios mio," and was ready for takeoff.

MAMI: Mira, mija, que linda las montañas . . .

MI: I opened my eyes to Mami pointing out the window—I expected to see water, I mean we were on an island, right? But I only saw miles and miles of majestic mountains below—deep, verdant mountains rose up and down and all around us. The beauty made me instantly dizzy with excitement and fear. I had to shut my eyes again. Mami began to sing.

MAMI: Yo soy jíbara, yo soy jíbara.

MI: I didn't know what that meant, but it sounded nice, so I started singing, too. (MI age 5) Yo soy jíbara . . . Mami, ¿qué es jíbara?

MAMI: Porque mi familia vive en el campo, son jíbaros.

MI: "Because my family lives in the country, they're country people." My cousin Ashley on my father's side later told me the real meaning for jíbaro was "peasant." The plane finally landed, rumbling to a halt. I opened my eyes, and unclenched my fists. My hands were bathed in melted Kisses. The ride from Ponce airport to Titi Caden's house was endless—I thought we were traveling to another country. The roads twisted and turned from pavement to dirt, we started seeing fewer houses and more trees. After nearly an hour, we were there. Titi Caden was waiting for us outside. She swept us into her arms, covering us with "Bienvenidos, la Bendición, mi familia!" It was almost like being home. Titi Caden didn't have hot water or a telephone, but she did have plenty of love, and a beautiful little next door neighbor. Marisol was my first crush . . . Marisol and me went to the beach everyday. We built sand castles, played in the water, held hands . . . she was so beautiful—a little darker than me, jet black curly long hair, big round eyes and a smile that made my heart giggle . . . I don't remember much more about that first trip to PR, except Titi Caden's delicious bacalao frito and Marisol . . . (Lights change.)

MAMI: Mija, Linky gave me five dollars to spend for your birthday—that's a dollar for every year! He said, "Mami, take her to Korvette's and buy her anything she wants—anything." So, now, mija, pick out whatever you want.

MI: I headed straight for the toy section. But just when my happy little hands reached OUT, Mami stepped IN:

MAMI: (looking around nervously) Mija, estos son boys' toys . . .

MI: I looked from my beloved prize and back to Mami's nervous eyes.

MAMI: Mija, you can have anything you want—(pointing) mira, mija, hay Barbie allí!

MI: But in those days, my fingers still had a mind and a heart of their own, so they clutched the beautiful bag of 100 cowboys and indians and wouldn't let go . . .

MAMI: Are you sure?

MI: I hugged the toy men closer to my chest—now I could play soldiers with my other brother! (nodding as child) "I'm sure! I'm ready to go home!"

MAMI: (shaking her head sadly) Ay, mija . . .

MI: Word spreads like a California wildfire in my family, courtesy of my titi's—within two hours I had a reputation . . .

TITI MAGDALENA: (sitting on SR chair) Iris, don't buy her a doll for Christmas unless it's GI Joe—the mother says she's playing with boys' toys, ¿tú sabes?

TITI IRIS: (sitting on SL chair) ¡Ay, no! ¡Qué pobrecita, la mama! (phoning Maria) María, Magdalena me dijó!

TITI MARIA: (standing SL) Ay, bendito, ¿qué pasó? She was such a beautiful little girl!

TITI IRIS: (sitting SL) Yo sé, and the way she always had her dressed to the nines! Pero, tú sabes, she has too many sons que her little girl don't know how to be a little girl!

TITI MARIA: (standing SL) Sí, sí, Christina, I'm telling you, Iris me dijó! She won't even look at a dress, goes into a tantrum every time the mother shows her a skirt! Sí, sí, the mother's in tears! Y she only plays con boys' toys, tú sabes!

TITI CRISTINA: (standing SR) Pués, if she was my daughter, I'da slapped the shit outta her!

MI: (crossing USL) I don't know where they got their information about the dresses—I didn't stop wearin' those 'til I was at least ten or eleven . . . as for the doll situation, I just couldn't—walkin' around with a doll, pretendin' it's your baby, feedin' it, burpin' it, changin' it; I mean, where's the entertainment value in that? (throws imaginary doll OSL) Now, Action Jackson and Big Jim—they were fun! Do you remember Big Jim, with the button you press in his back to make him do karate chops? Man, that was exciting! (jumping on cube) Or, how about Evel Knievel with his battery operated motorcycle, poppin' wheelies and jumpin' ramps . . . I used to love buildin' ramps just to see how high he could go before he fell off the bike (jumps off cube) . . . yeah, those were dolls I could get into . . . I thought Mami took it in stride, but I caught her crying, so I began collecting Malibu Barbie and Skipper, too (with their tans they could almost pass for Puerto Rican). They went campin' with the guys and they would all climb mountains . . . but, since Malibu Barbie and Skipper only had their bathing suits, I let them wear GI Joe's clothes—hey, you can't climb mountains in bikinis! (Lights change. She sits on SR chair, legs up.) No amarillos . . . no coquito . . . no rice and beans . . . only in my mami's kitchen once a week . . . no matter how often we visited New York, it was always a day too short . . . I missed the Bronx and my brother, Linky, who stayed behind . . . pués, he was 19 and he had a good job with Manny Hanny; I was 7 and had no voice . . . no choice . . . and no idea how much I really missed my native New York. It was a slow kind of missing—I stayed "con la gana," with the yearning . . . it's the kind of missing that never dies; not even the act of forgetting can kill it. You can forget a memory, but not a feeling, not a sense, not a smell . . . See, in New York, we didn't go to church on Sunday, we went to Yankee Stadium! And Orchard Beach—ahhh, a day at Orchard Beach was a day in heaven! The juicy scents of mami's pollo frito and Coppertone lotion, the majestic sounds of a thousand portable radios blastin' Tito Puente . . . my Uncle Raymond takin' me to the Bronx Zoo or White Castle or just hangin' out and turnin' me on to the latest Jackson Five hit . . . tú sabes, the kids in Connecticut didn't even know who Michael Jackson was—they were into Donny Osmond . . . I've never thought of my family as middle class, although to our old friends from the Bronx, moving to Connecticut meant we had "made it" . . . what I wanna know is what exactly did we make? And where did we make it to? We may have made it out of the Bronx, but we were still working class . . . shit, in Connecticut we still didn't have a garage or a dishwasher! Middle class . . . the kids I went to school with complained that they were only middle class—coño, to me, having a two-car garage, two-story house, two acres of land and three closets full of L.L. Bean was filthy rich! They made me think we were poverty stricken. (Music cue: Donny Osmond's "Go Away Little Girl." She hopscotches US, crossing L to RS wall.) Jeanette DiPatria. Italiana. A year older than me and born in the Bronx, too. They'd moved to Connecticut before us, so she'd already lost her accent. I didn't even know I had an accent, until Jeanette and her brother, Joey, kept laughing at me every time I said 'orange soder.' After several weeks of their intense drilling, I learned to say 'orange soda' and other words just like them. Mami and papi speak perfect English when they think I'm listening . . . the little Spanish I knew, I didn't know what to do with . . . it's not that it wasn't allowed in the house, it just wasn't encouraged . . . so, in seventh grade, I took Spanish, bringing in all the catch phrases that I had picked up at home . . . but, I didn't realize there's a big difference between Castillian—what we learned in school— and Puerto Rican Spanish. (pounding wall) I flunked the first couple of vocabulary tests, mostly 'cause I couldn't spell. And I kept arguing with my teacher about the existence of non-existent words like 'perate, a 'mimir o pow-pow, and coñocarajo. I hated school.

(crossing to CS) They didn't teach
Angela Davis
Or
María Irene Fornes
Or
Tillie Olsen
Or
Sonia Sanchez
In my Connecticut

Public High School—
We were lucky enough
To get a taste of
Lorraine Hansberry and Lillian Hellman—

And they didn't teach
Me
What to do
(crossing DSC) With my Latina lesbian hands
Holding an American pen
At that New
England
School

1979 and I had cried
Myself to sleep
At least one-hundred eighty-five nights
that sophomore year
Never knowing why
no amarillos
no coquito
no rice and beans
only in my mami's kitchen
once a week

So I wrote
With a secret pen
Closet writer
Closet case
Closet Puerto Rican
And hated Monday mornings
And dated
Boys
And loved
Girls—
But only in my journal.

And learning how to paint
my straight girl face
was as easy as learning how to paint
the Sistine Chapel
without a palette

I dated boys.
I loved girls,
But only in my journal.
(crosses to SR chair and sits) 1980, and I, half-waiting
For Mr.Right,
Wondered what it would be like
To salsa with Elena or Kate
Instead of José or Biff.

Junior prom came
And went
Without Mi—
I was home, alone,
In my closet,
The sweet refuge
Of Papi's hand-me-down boxers and pajamas,
Writing and
Dreaming of Elena and Kate and Marisol and Grace—
I dreamed I was their date

Merengue, cha-cha, hustle, salsa, bump
And grind . . .
Lips to lips,
Breasts to breasts,
Eye to eye . . .
I didn't really know how
to dance, but in my mind,
in my closet,
in my spaghetti straps—
in my mind, I wore
stiletto heels,

it was so fly
I didn't even feel
the sting of the WASPs

in my mind,
I did not hide . . .

The idea of Queen and Queen
Of the Prom
stayed with me the rest of the year.

(cross to CS, march DS, shake hands) 1981, Graduation's here
And who gives a flying fuck
When they're force-feeding us
Reagan?
(chucks diploma) I stopped dating boys
That June
(crosses DSL and kneels on chair) 1982, and I fell in love
With you
And gave birth
To the secret thoughts
that, until then, had resigned themselves
To the permanent residence IN
side my head.

Yet Mami said
IT
Was a
SIN.

So, I started dating
Boys again. (Lights change. She sits on DSL chair with back to audience,
stomping feet.) 4 years, 12 flings, 2 boyfriends and 1 lesbian experience
later, I escaped to New York. (She runs USC.)

Voices in the night
Or day, my own

People sayin'
"You're so white!" or
"You're so straight"
"Gringa, Blanquita"
"La Niña Bonita!" they
Tuck me
In
Under a blanket of
In
Security . . .

(slowly crossing DS) A Puerto Rican Sister
Pushin' time
Shares, condos
On this Isla Verde beach
As fast
And slow
As dope
My Sister, lighter
Than me
Has the huevos
To speak, "You must
Have some of that pure
European blood
In you, like me!"

"I'm not like you!"
I think. I
Think, "Who would
Want more
Of her so-called
Pure, European
Blood that contaminated
History with trans
Fusions of Imperialism?
Conquistadores—Conquerors
Conquering, Raped

A People, A Land and A
Culture." I think.

So disarmed by my
Thoughts and fear,

How can I
Let the words
Out? "Nenita,
Tenemos todos
En mi familia!"
"We have every color
Of the rainbow and more in
My family, honey!"
I suddenly shout.

I am a
Puerto Rican Lesbian, I think.
But I'm tired.
So tired of having
To defend
My light skin
My Anglo-looking face
My New England education
My accent-less accent
My Spanglish-laden Spanish
My long straight hair
And my flat, flat ass
To voices in the night
Or day, my own
People
(pointing to audience) And you,
Tired. (She crosses to SR chair and curls up in fetal position on chair.)

I am so tired that I don't remember the exact moment I got IN—it's all a
blur . . . one moment I was chopping sofrito for my girlfriend's omelette—
one moment I was loving her, one moment I was loving my Self, and the

next, I was OUT . . . I was OUT, but not really OUT . . . I mean I was OUT, like a light . . . OUT like a light on the deconstructed Bruckner Express-way.. (Tangos with straitjacket.)

At 22, I still had la gana for New York. (rising, crosses USL) So, I up-rooted my Self from Connecticut to blossom in Manhattan's Upper East Side . . . the Upper East Side? What was I looking for there? The only Puerto Ricans were nannies and doormen. There were no lesbians and no rice and beans at the Food Emporium—coño, you couldn't even get plátanos for at least thirty blocks! So, I fled to Brooklyn. In Carroll Gardens, I found the flower of my dreams, Maya. She was the first Puerto Rican-Dominican I had ever met. I couldn't resist her long-as-Crystal Gale's hair which I soon found out was a weave (feels and drops hair). A year later, I still hadn't found my roots or hers, so, I moved (hopscotches to DSL corner) from Brooklyn to Chelsea to Staten Island and ended up in Hoboken, New Jer-sey . . . funny thing was, 'though, I found a lot of Latinos . . . only I couldn't speak to them . . .

(leaning against wall) All is
Not fair
In Food and Beverage
You tell me
As one of your co-workers—one
Of my Latino brothers—repeatedly
Stabs you with the butcher
Knife of ignorance
"I heard a dirty rumor, I heard a
Dirty rumor—I heard you don't like men!"
He jabs.
"Is it true, is it true, you're into
Women?" the taunting tone
Demands.
Somebody saw us kiss
Last Friday morning
When I dropped you off
At work
Somebody saw us
Somebody saw

Us some
Body saw us
Kiss
When I dropped

Your heart
Plops
To the chopping block
The knife twists
Prime cut
Roast rump
He craves
To slice
It up

Your mouth
Is raw
With anger
And fear
"I'll fuck anything
That walks!" is all
You can retort.

He turns on
His meat
Grinder and blender
Simultaneously.

"Why you like that? Why
You like that? Why, you?" he asks
Incredulously.
Licking his lips, his eyes affixed
On your breasts, he secretly
Desires to puree, strain
And taste test.

But other customers await.
Your co-worker zips up
His machismo and
Walks away.
This time.

(crossing to DSL chair, kneels) At home
Alone,
You cry first
All the words you could not say to him,
Then, pick up the phone
And dial me.

In a calmer state of mind
You surmise, "It all comes down to pride—
If they can't control or fuck you, they don't
Want to deal!"
But your next breath
Remembers the fear.
"Maybe I should just get married and have kids!"

My heart
Momentarily
Plops
To the chopping block,
Then springs back
Into place.

"You could marry me
And have kids!" I boldly state.

"Really?"

"Yeah, really. But some
Homophobe
Saw us kiss
Last Friday morning,

So, I'll drop you off
At the corner,
And kiss you
At home."

(sitting) "I'm too white for the Spanish kids, and too Spanish for the white kids," my 16-year old niece told me one day. I was so relieved she was telling me this over the phone, because I didn't want her to see the hurt in my face, the pain in my ears, hearing history repeat itself. But silence is painful, too, so before it got too painfully quiet, I spoke up: "Me, too, mija, me, too."

(Lights change. She rises, crosses US, picks up boom box and crosses DR.)

MI: Hola, Mami, la Bendición. (Sets down boom box on cube. Kisses imaginary figure of Mami.)

MI: ¿Cómo estás? How's your sugar? Good . . . What're you doing? You wanna sit up more? Here, lemme help—okay! I was just trying—está bien . . . con calma, tranquila . . . oye, Mami, I brought the CD's you wanted . . . remember? You asked me to bring Tito, Willie, Joe Cuba y—c'mon, you remember, "Hazlo, hazlo, hazlo!" Check it out . . . (Sound cue: as she presses button on boom box, Joe Cuba's *Bang, Bang* plays.)

MI: Mami, mira . . . when we lived in the Bronx, Evergreen and Story Ave.? No, '64 . . . the hazlo chair! I know that's not what it's really called, but that's what you called it, 'cause every time you put me in that baby walker, you put on a Joe Cuba record and shouted, "Hazlo, hazlo, hazlo!"

(Sound cue: as she turns off boom box, *Bang, Bang* stops. She sits in DR chair.)

Tú sabes, the authorities are recallin' those walkers now . . . for real! They claim it's a health hazard for babies, saying it stunts their growth and doesn't allow them to touch their feet the way they're supposed to. Well, babies don't need to be touchin' their feet all the time, anyway, that's a lotta germs. Yeah, and they said too many parents are using the hazlo chair as a baby sitter. Man, don't they know? The hazlo chair was my first dance teacher! Next to you, claro que sí. (standing) Remember, Mami? You in your black capris pants and sleeveless turtleneck, with your hair in that crazy upsweep? "¡Hazlo! ¡Hazlo! ¡Baila pa' Mami! Dance for Mami, Cuca!" (MI dances down center.)

Yeah, I kept dancing for you, 'til I was about seven. No, no, I had been out of the hazlo chair for nearly five or six years by then . . . I graduated to the new stage you created for me: the center of our living room. You made me entertain whenever we had company . . . until Papi got a promotion and we moved to Connecticut . . . then you made me go to ballet . . . and I hated it! Trying to keep my leg on that ridiculous bar, forced to listen to that boring, music! Where was Joe Cuba? You said, "No hay Joe Cuba! You're going to be a ballerina!" (Sound cue: Swan Lake.)

"The first Puerto Rican in the Nutcracker!" Because I wanted to run and jump! Oh, yeah, ballerinas run and jump, into the arms of un maricón! No, I suffered, three times a week, for six weeks, con esa bruja, Miss Rivinska.

(Mi crosses to CS, begins leg extensions.)

MISS RIVINSKA: (Russian accent) Ex-tend! Ex-tend! Ex-tend, ex-tend, ex-tend! 2-3-4-5—Miss Ass-tor, keep holding! Miss Ass-tor, you will never be swan at this rate! Miss Ass-tor, when I have stop for you, you make entire class fall behind! Miss Ass-tor, you're dragging everyone down with you! Let's go! 2-3-4-5-6-7-8! Ex-tend! Ex-tend! Ex-tend, ex-tend, ex—

MI: (dropping leg to stand) I'm tired!

MISS RIVINSKA: You think Nijinska ever said tired?

MI: Hell, yeah! (Sound cue: Swan Lake stops abruptly.)
MI: The room full of blonde hair and blue eyes were like ping-pongs, bobbing their gaze between Miss Rivinska and me.

MISS RIVINSKA: Miss Ass-tor, remove self from this class immediately!

MI: What are you talkin' about? You did not have to beg her to take me back the next week. I saw you slip her the extra fifty! Yeah, I went back—

armed. I slipped in early, way before Miss Rivinska had arrived—I was by the window, pretending to be stretching with the brown-nosers. As soon as I saw her come in through the main entrance, I left the bar. I knew I still had a minute before she made it up the five flights of stairs. I ran over to the record player, and unleashed my ammo. (Sound cue: Joe Cuba's *Bang, Bang* blares. Mi dances.) Some of the cooler girls giggled. The wimps just glared. But I didn't care! I was back in the Bronx, entertaining our familia! (Sound Cue: *Bang, Bang* stops abruptly.) Miss Rivinska yanked my Joe Cuba record off the turntable! (Sound Cue: *Theme from Charlie's Angels* as MI does a series of karate kicks, spins, steps and kicks Miss Rivinska.) I guess all that work on the bar paid off, 'cause when my leg made contact, the bitch went flyin'! I'm sorry, Mami, but she was a bitch! Boom! Smack on her flat, snobby ass! Well, you couldn't have been that mad, 'cause you didn't yell at me in Spanish. ¿Y qué? You sure didn't look like an American citizen a week later when you were gettin' down with Papi at the Spanish-American club dance. In Co-op City, remember? You two were the Puerto Rican Rogers and Astaire. (crossing USC) When you took the floor – and, I mean, you took the floor—it was magic . . . (leaning against US wall) the music really came alive, and I felt like I was part of this new world you had created, where congas and timbales and trumpets ruled, where music became a secret language which only you and Papi understood completely . . . your dancing was the translation, but I struggled to understand. It was so hard because I didn't know where to keep my eyes, or my ears . . . so much fervor and excitement . . . so much joy and spirit! How I longed to be like you! But, I always had to go home, to Connecticut, to my friends . . . I tried turning them on to Joe Cuba, but they laughed. And, sometimes I laughed, too. They were into Led Zeppelin. I don't know how anyone can dance to Stairway to Heaven, but la pendeja que yo soy, I tried – I had to: that was the last song at every junior high and high school dance. Practice? Where? At the town's annual Bavarian Beer Festival, where the biggest number was the polka? Mami, mira, I know you and Papi did your best, but . . . I never felt right in that fuckin' little hick town . . . okay, I promise I won't curse anymore, pero, coño, Mami, I lost a lot more than my rhythm when we moved to Connecticut . . . with hair down to my culo and my Frida Kahlo eyebrow and thick Bronx accent, the kids didn't know what to make of me . . . yeah, well, I may be light, but they were white, next to them I looked like friggin' Pocahontas and sounded like Al Pacino. Then, whenever we visited the Bronx, Uncle Pepo kept tellin' me how I spoke English like a Connecticut Yankee. Then you tellin' me I spoke Spanish like a Jew ... oh, sí, you did! Mami, I just ... I was too Spanish for the white kids, and too white for the Spanish kids ... Slowly, but surely, I started to lose my rhythm. And a Puerto Rican girl without rhythm, that's oxymoronic, yo! ¡Qué desgracia! Fuckin' tragic is what it is! Uncle Ray tried to help me get it back by teaching me salsa and merengue at the occasional family wedding, but, I would get so nervous, thinkin' everybody was gonna laugh at me ... my body would freeze up ... So, I haven't set foot on a dance floor in ... years. I can't. Deep down, I still love Joe Cuba, but I've got this thing, now. Ay, yo no sé. An affliction. Paralysis. My legs are connected to my spirit connected to my mind connected to the memory of constantly being told I can't dance. It's true—girlfriends, choreographers, colleagues. They've all said it, some, to my face! The sympathetic ones whisper about me to each other, "¡Ay, bendito!" Mami, life was so much simpler in the hazlo chair days ... no pressure, no phobias. No afflictions. No diabetes. (beat) I'm sorry, I ... mira, I'd better go, visiting hours are almost ... over ... I love you.

(She kisses imaginary Mami. Lights fade on DR area. Lights come up on CS chair, as Mi sits.) Mami lost her battle with diabetes; but she put up a vivacious front, fighting the debilitating disease for almost 20 years. Strokes, neuropathy—nerve damage—chiseled away at her mind and body ... Papi tried to care for her at home – no dancing floors, just molded shoes, syringes, gluco strips and a walker ... then, a hospital bed, hand splints, diapers, catheter, and finally, a nursing home, and amputation of the right leg. And even though Papi was beginning to show signs of his own degenerative illness—Parkinson's—and the tremors got so bad sometimes he couldn't shave for days—he literally stayed by Mami's side, every day, trying to stop her hands from curling into themselves. Massaging, caressing, stroking, holding, kissing her—he was still her dance partner, 'til the very end. On my last visit with Mami, I brought her a Marc Anthony CD. I thought it would reawaken her Puerto Rican pride to know that a new generation is appreciating, creating, and re-creating the sounds we've always loved. (As MI crosses DR, lights fade up.) ¿Qué qué? Since when did you stop listening to Spanish music? C'mon, Mami ... It makes me want to dance, too. Dance for you, Mami. Whenever I hear Marc, Tito, Willie, Eddie and La India, I'm transported back—to the Spanish-American club dances at Co-op City, to the family weddings, to Joe Cuba and the hazlo chair. And maybe, just maybe all we need is the magic of those memories to reclaim our rhythm . . . (Sound cue: *Bang, Bang* fades up, then full. MI begins to slowly find her rhythm.)

¡Baila pa' Cuca, Mami! C'mon! Yes, you can, just take my hand . . . let me dance for you, Mami . . . I'll try to pick up where you left off. ¡Hazlo! ¡Hazlo! ¡Hazlo! (Sound cue: *Bang, Bang* ends. Lights change.)

(MI crosses US) I came back to New York, 98th and Amsterdam. Muchos Dominicanos por alli, and I felt almost at home, but . . . I could walk into a restaurant and order carne guisa' or café con leche, but I couldn't carry on a conversation beyond "¿comó estás?" I saw a sign for mondongo and thought they had misspelled mofongo, mashed green plantains, but I found out too late that the tripe soup in front of me was definitely not mofongo. Tho' I found sanctuary in a Chelsea convent for three years, I didn't become a lesbian nun—that would've been redundant . . . I had met a wonderful woman, not at the convent—her name was Estrella— that means star—we were together five years . . . Estrella's not really Spanish, she's African American, but she feels Spanish because her parents conceived her in Cuba. That's what she says. Our first Christmas together, I was really poor. But I saw these earrings that I knew she had to have. (crosses SR) It was Christmas Eve and the guy sellin' 'em on Bleecker and Broadway was just about to close up shop . . . I reached into my pocket and pulled out all I had left: four tokens and a dollar . . . he let me keep the dollar . . . He first mistook me for a WASP.

"They're African seeds," He tells me
With pride and sincerity
For a smile

"I made them myself—
You know African seeds?"
He asks, gently holding
A pair
Near, still
Smiling
Through the wind chill

Factor, twenty below
And counting

'Africa flows
In my Puerto Rican
Blood,' I think while
Returning the smile
And almost whispering
My reply, "Yes, I
Know African seeds."
But on the verge
Of my quivering lips
Lives
Another Truth—
Words that can
Not escape
The Prison of Fear;

In
Com
Plete
Sen
Ten
Ces

Born from
Over-zealous thoughts—
Once fallen on deaf ears—
Delivered C-Section—
I had to cut, I had
To cut, I had to
Censor Myself

Although I know
Self-imposed silence
Is the worst kind
Of noise

I had to shut, I had
To shut, I had to
Lock the gate
To my cell, to my
Self, just
In case he also mis
Took me
For something else

When all I really wanted
To do
Was tell the brother
How
I know
African seeds
How
I have felt
Africa beating
In my lover's heart
How
My lover
Is

A Woman
An African-American
Woman
Woman

Of color
Of Soweto
Of Sahara
Of Kalahari
Of Kwanzaa
Of Fulani
Of Mandela
Of Malcolm
Of King

Of Niger
Of Savannah
Of Green
And Red
And Yellow
And Gold . . .

Beyond this pale
Olive skin,
Lives a Puerto Rican
Sista
Loving your earrings,
Brother,

Loving your African seeds
Loving them so much
But not loving my
Self enough
To tell you
They're not for me,
They're for my lover . . . (She sits DL.)

I regret coming out to my mother on the phone. We should have been at her kitchen table, sharing a pot of Quietly Chamomile . . . but, hey, "long distance," the next best thing to bein' there, right?

MAMI: So you're published . . . that's good, pero qué es eso, "OUTWEEK?"

MI: It's a . . . weekly news magazine . . . for . . . for the, the lesbian and gay community . . .

MAMI: (long pause) And why are you writing for them?

MI: Pués, I've always been supportive, tú sabes, of, of, of their, their, causes, their—

MAMI: Are you thinking you might be one of them?

MI: No, Mami, I don't think . . . I know . . . I am a lesbian . . .

MAMI: (crying) ¡Ay, qué terible, qué horible! I should've never let you shave with your father!

MI: And although she didn't utter another word, behind every tear I could hear Mami's runaway train of thought: "I should've never let you join Little League! Or build forts in the woods! Or wear your father's pajamas! I should've never bought you the GI Joes . . . " (setting up three chairs DSL) A week later, I went home to celebrate my 27th birthday . . . Mami always baked me a cake, but I was afraid she wasn't bakin' me one this time . . . Papi picked me up at the bus station—he was so happy, no way she could have told him. He hugged me for so long, like he didn't wanna let go . . . and the forty minute drive to the house, I thought it would be the longest ride of my life, but, it went by much too fast . . . Papi talked to me, I mean, really talked to me—not just about George Steinbrenner, but about Puerto Rican politics! We get there, Mami's waiting at the door. But she's all smiles. We have all my favorites—Mami's pollo frito y arroz con garbanzos . . . homemade yellow cake with chocolate icing . . . we laugh, we drink champagne . . . they sing "Happy Birthday" to me, and we watch TV together . . . yo no sé, GOLDEN GIRLS or HART TO HART . . . next morning, Mami and I are up at five . . . and just as I'm pouring two cups of Quietly Chamomile, Mami jumps up.

MAMI: (waving her finger) Okay, now we're gonna talk about your problem. And I don't care what you say, but it has everything to do with your ex-boyfriend, Biff! Your father has cried himself to sleep every night this week . . . "Pero, gracías a Dios," he says through his tears, "At least she's not a junkie or a prostitute . . ."

MI: (to Mami) I was seeing Biff but writing poetry for Cheryl! (to audience) Apparently, Biff wasn't the only victim of Mami's blame game. My father became convinced that allowing me to wear his hand-me-down boxers and pajamas is what really turned me into a lesbian. So, he promptly stopped giving me his hand-me-downs, and pretty soon, he even stopped wearing boxers and switched to briefs. (She begins marching and lining up chairs from DSL to USL, chanting) 2-4-6-8, how do you know your kid's not straight? 2-4-6-8, how do you know your kid's not straight? 2-4-6-8, how do you know your kid's not straight? Six years later, summer of '96 – first time I marched in a Gay Pride Parade. I had always been on the sidelines, 34th & 5th, with my Uncle Ray. Him and his picnic basket – empanadillas, bacalao frito, flan, those little cans of guava nectar . . . and my favorite, Dipsey Doodles . . . but this was the first summer without my Uncle Ray . . . after the march, I felt so exhausted and exhilarated . . . and, sad . . . (sitting in chair) I collapsed on my couch . . . the phone rang . . . it was Mami . . . I was terrified, because, I hadn't told her I was marching, and part of me wanted to, but the other part—

MAMI: Cuca, how you doing?

MI: Fine, Mami, I'm fine.

MAMI: Oye, your father has something to tell you . . . (calling to Papi) honey, ven acá, I got her on the phone . . .

MI: Oh, shit . . . what the hell—

PAPI: ¿Nena?

MI: Hey, Papi

PAPI: Were you marching in the Gay parade today?

MI: Uh—

PAPI: With the Puerto Rican flag wrapped around your head?

MI: Uh, well, it was a bandana, Papi . . .
PAPI: I knew it was you! (to Mami) You see, honey, I knew it was her!

MAMI: (to Papi) I knew it was her, too, I just couldn't see for sure, I didn't have my glasses! You tryin' to tell me I don't know my own daughter? (calling to Mi) You looked beautiful, nena!

PAPI: I tried to tape it, but by the time I got the video, you were gone! But don't worry, mija, I'm gonna watch the 10 and 11 o'clock news, they gotta play it again, and I'll get it then!

MI: They sounded so happy and proud . . . as proud as I felt in the parade, (kneeling CS) when thousands of us laid our bodies down, an endless stream on the city streets, to remember Uncle Ray and all the others we lost to AIDS. It was a great day . . . I never want to lose that feeling . . . I just want . . . more great days . . .

Nights
I love to lie awake
Watching her,
My wife,
As she sleeps
And get lost
in her essence
mesmerized by the rise
and fall of her breasts

The sweet scent of her
Pachouli and cocoa butter
Beckoning me closer
Feeling her skin, soft smooth brown
more luminous than the moon against the midnight sky
Skin
Crimson lips honeysuckle luscious, in motion from
Moan dream or breath . . .

We are in Connecticut
In our house
In our upstairs bedroom
With the slanted ceilings
And crackling walls we so lovingly painted
And proudly decorated—

This is where I feel safe
This is where I belong

This is home
Our home

The paper says civil union
But our hearts minds souls, the JOP, 100 friends and family say
    MARRIED!

Who has the right to legislate love? to state
We are good enough to vote, to teach, to counsel, to pay taxes
To die
for our country but
Not to marry? (She interacts with the straitjacket.)

Yeah, I returned to Connecticut—for love. Funny how love for my Self got me out of Connecticut, and love for a woman brought me back. One moment I was demonstrating in front of the office of the Puerto Rican Commonwealth, protesting Regulation 87—the mandatory reporting of HIV and AIDS—and the next, I was living in Connecticut, being inducted into the local Rotary club, singing "My Country 'Tis of Thee," and pledging allegiance to a country I don't recognize anymore, for it certainly doesn't recognize me, or my human right to marry the woman of my dreams. "Sweet land of liberty . . . " One moment I was immersed in the sea of coquis, rainbows and salsa floats rippling into El Barrio, and the next, I was listening to a Rotary sister warn me I could tell the club I was Puerto Rican but I should stay silent about my sexuality. "Of thee I sing . . . " One moment I was Vice-President of the Puerto Rican Initiative to Develop Empowerment, and the next, I was one of a handful of women in a roomful of white-haired white men, thinking, as white as my skin is, I still don't blend in . . . "Land where my fathers died, land of the pilgrims' pride . . . " But then, I remember, last year, two days before Thanksgiving, as I joined Rotary members, smiling through bitter cold and sleet, delivering hundreds of turkeys to the underprivileged . . . how proud I felt to be part of a club that has raised thousands of dollars for college scholarships, food pantries and other worthy causes . . .

I remember this, and ask myself, "Why do I need to blend in; can't I just be me?" "From every mountain side, let freedom ring . . . "

I don't remember
the exact moment
I got IN

it
could have been
the moment
Mami scolded me,
Pulling her hands
through my man—
tailored buzz cut

it could have been
the moment
Jesse Helms
tried to shut
my lesbian fingers
up

or, maybe it
was when
the nation deemed immigration its curse,
bilingual, an official dirty word—
(tangos with jacket) it could have been
the moment
my girl
friend
told me
I danced
like a
white chick . . .

or maybe it was when
a New York City critic
said I was miscast
in my autobiography . . .

Magdalena Gómez and *María Luisa Arroyo*   169

I don't remember
the exact moment

I got IN

but it
could have been
it could have been
when
I started
buyin' in
to this shit! (She throws straitjacket US. Lights change.)

MI: I started writing plays when I was nine. Me and my cousins performed them at our Tita's house in Castle Hill. The Bronx, between the projects and the river, great view of the Whitestone Bridge. Val and me played dope addicts, the other cousins were neighborhood big shots—crooked cops, drug lords, deadbeat dads, welfare cheats. Val's 7-year old sister was our alcoholic sidekick, Chicky. I don't know why—maybe I had some sick fascination with their desperation. Or maybe I was just so used to being fed those images. But, my writing has evolved. And I've done pretty well for myself—although, sometimes, I look at Rosie Perez or J Lo and I think, 'maybe I haven't done that well . . . maybe I haven't suffered enough . . . if only I had pelo malo, if only I had been a shade darker . . . if only I had stayed in the Bronx, kept my accent, gotten a white girl's perm, joined a gang—I could've passed for a light-skinned Puerto Rican and been a star!' I'm sure I would've had a feature film or two under my belt by now—probably co-starring Jessica Lange as the adoptive mother of my illegitimate child or Michelle Pfeiffer as my sympathetic but tough-as-nails ESL teacher . . . or, Al Pacino as my drug-dealing big brother . . . or, Miriam Colón as my mother, the maid! I guess I'm just not marketable enough . . . but "I coulda been a contenda!" (Beat.) I don't remember the exact moment I got IN—it's all a blur . . . one moment I am chopping sofrito for my wife's omelette—one moment I am loving her, one moment I am loving my Self, and the next, I am OUT . . . I am OUT, really OUT . . . I mean I am OUT! (She exits through the audience. Blackout.)

    END OF PLAY

Diego Angarita-Horowitz

Making Homophobia Visible

It looks like:
3rd grade in front of the blackboard
us sitting in a semi-circle learning about rhyming words
wooden chairs, short tables with green yellow blue red tops
stay, pray, day, hay, lay, way,
Any more my teacher asks?
GAY, I say
She cringes, as the class bursts into laughter
they all look at me
because they know
because they KNOW
because THEY know
Don't you even know what that means?
he says

It looks like:
5th grade, Rainy day
We have a substitute
It's recess and we stay indoors
I'm bored and have no one to play with
I walk over to HIM playing checkers.
Can I play with you guys? I ask
NO, HE says. You're a queer.
I walk away guilty of being ignorant
Not knowing that word.
I ask my mom when I get home what that word means
Her face freezes. Let's check the dictionary, she says.
I avoid eye contact, already suspecting the definition
www.merriamwebsterdictionary.com
1 a : worthless, counterfeit <queer money>
b : questionable, suspicious
2 a : differing in some odd way from what is usual or normal b (1) :
    eccentric, unconventional (2) : mildly insane : touched c : absorbed

or interested to an extreme or unreasonable degree: obsessed d (1) often
    disparaging : homosexual (2) sometimes offensive : gay 4b
Where did you hear it?
HE called me one.
Well maybe he meant that you're an individual.
I'm mortified. No mom he didn't. It's ok. I get what he was saying

It looks like:
6th grade stock market game
all the kids of Yale professors and doctors
learning about finances
Can I be a part of the game?
No HE says you're too:
short
dark
queer
gay
stupid
lazy
young
ugly
girlie
quiet
All the kids who played the game
ended up going to ivy league schools
big surprise they're all white

It looks like:
7th grade, at the bus stop
My hair any color but black
My clothes, a costume
because I have to perform everyday
Whiteness
Straightness
Male
and I'm so bad at it.
Everyday I have to run home

because SHE chases me
come back here, you PANSY
You fuckin' Faggot
I'm going to kick your ass
when I catch you
Finally one day I've had enough
I don't run anymore.
She swings and misses
I grab her ear full of multicolored earrings
I pull her to the ground and step on her face
Don't you ever come after me again
or I'll rip your earrings out

It looks like:
8th grade
We get days off for
snow days
floods
broken heating
Parent teacher conferences
Bomb threats
There are two kinds of boys
the bleached hair blond boys
who walk around yelling faggot
listening to eminem on their discmans
ready to kill any faggot or queer they find
I see them
I see the BOYS and I see the Faggots
I don't open my mouth because they will see me
The other kind of boys dress in black listen to
Marilyn Manson and make hit lists
They call in bomb threats

It looks like:
9th grade sex ed class
Matthew Shepard on the news
and no one talks about it

I saw him on MTV
Dancing to britney spears in NYC
on TRL Gerald
So visible and out
To be mocked and abused
Then disappeared
I see them with multicolored hair
and manicured hands
and shaped eyebrows
facial piercings
they gradually grow more visible
then disappear
into the night
beaten out of the daylight
into night school GED classes
where they can be invisible
and safe
I can't go to night school
I have to get into college
So I make myself more invisible

It looks like:
10th grade
my best friends from 6th grade
and this girl I don't know
calling me faggot in front of the whole school
2400 students
my best friends from 6th grade
calling me faggot
I sit with the ESL kids at lunch
they don't know those words yet
They don't understand what they mean
I'm learning Spanish
They don't call me faggot.
wait
Marica maricín puto viado
but they call me

blanco
gringo
I'm learning Spanish

It looks like:
11th grade
Spanish for Spanish speaker classes
not offered on an honors level
celebrating multi-culturalism
with all white honors classes
teachers checking off race stats in AP class
Mike, you're egyptian right?
I'm going to put you down as pacific islander.
That's it, right. No one else here is
black? hispanic? asian? native?
Connecticut Mastery Test
my race box already checked off as white
I've been in honors classes my whole life
as if they know I'll score well
score for THEIR team
being sent to diversity team building
to mediate the brown kids
getting called a faggot by
this white girl in the back of the bus
who's in foster care

It looks like:
12th grade, taking over the GSA
organizing teacher awareness training
attending youth conferences
using my voice
losing friends
making my gay visible
making my brown visible
finding allies in unlikely places
having dangerous sex
because no one ever taught

me to be safe
or what that even looked like
meeting men online
so many questions
finding my own answers
in the streets of NYC
on the beach, in the clubs
in parking lots
because I never had anyone
show me what healthy
looked like

Yolanda Maria-Rose Scavron

Confessions of a Gay Basher

I can still taste his blood in my mouth. Hear his screams in my ears. Feel . . . feel my hands pound his flesh. See . . . I . . . oh God. I can still see his face . . . torn. Ripped apart. Flayed. Yeah, that's the word. Flayed. Like in those pictures after a lion finishes its food . . . yeah . . . I can still see that. I'm so glad they don't know about me. They almost did. That day. Five seconds earlier and it would have been me instead of him. That look in Richie's eyes. I knew that look. I'd seen it before. He was gonna kill that kid. Gonna? He did kill that kid . . . we all did . . . I did. You know, you'd think that would be the part that keeps me up most nights. But it's not. The way their necks snapped round so fast . . . the look in my brother's eyes. The way my best friend's hands balled into fists. The way my dad seemed so proud when he found out what we had done. That . . . that's what keeps me up at night. Knowing. Not thinking, but knowing that if they found out about me. If they knew . . . if they knew I was . . . . that I liked . . . that I'm . . . that I'm . . . well let's just say, in my culture, it's unacceptable for a man to fall in love . . . .with another man.

Diego Angarita-Horowitz

Yes, HOMO!

I just have to say aloud
because I love my body
because I'm responsible
because I'm not a victim
because I'm educated
Yes, Yes, Homo! Yes, Yes, Homo!

I have to call it out now
because I learn from my past
because I listen to my elders
because I share with the youth
because I believe in a healthy future
Yes, Yes, Homo! Yes, Yes, Homo!
Yes, Yes, Homo! Yes, Yes, Homo!

I need to break the silence
because I have integrity
because I'm a badass artist
because I don't give my power
because I believe in community
Yes, Yes, Homo! Yes, Yes, Homo!
Yes, Yes, Homo! Yes, Yes, Homo!

I want everyone to see me
because I exist and you'd better respect me
because I have a heart and I'm sensitive
because I'm done being silent
because it's about time for a new masculinity
Yes, Yes, Homo! Yes, Yes, Homo!
Yes, Yes, Homo! Yes, Yes, Homo!

I need you to pay attention
because I'm a survivor
because I'm boy crazy
because I'm anti-violence
because I'm pro peace
Yes, Yes, Homo! Yes, Yes, Homo!
Yes, Yes, Homo! Yes, Yes, Homo!

Cathy J. Schlund-Vials

Memory

The following is a story I have told to no one. I am seven years old. I think I am in the second grade. Or, perhaps I am in the first grade. The lack of certainty troubles me.

Not for the reasons you would expect—as someone five years from forty, I am used to not remembering the specifics of three decades. It is a remembrance that inconveniently makes itself visible when I enter a room filled with people I don't know. It is there when I speak. It is present when I move through the world. It is a thought that won't leave quietly. Instead, it loudly reminds me of a lowness, what Martin Luther King most famously observed as a profound sense of "nobodiness." Its effect therefore should be matched by clarity—not vagueness—of remembrance.

This is what I do remember. I remember grays, whites, and dark blues. At the time, I was living in England. My father was career military—Air Force to be more precise—which meant that we would move, move, move. Born in Thailand, we moved to Florida. From Florida we moved to England. From England we moved to Georgia. From Georgia we moved to Texas. Of all the places, however, it was the brief time spent in England—perhaps three or four years—that left its permanent mark.

American author Toni Morrison once said (and I paraphrase) that every person of color remembers that time. My time came with Lisa, a girl with brown hair, shoulder length, a nose spotted and dotted with freckles. I don't remember why we were friends. Perhaps it was the proximity of a desk. Or maybe it was an identical colored notebook or shared giggle. Regardless, we were, for at least two weeks, best friends in the way kids are quickly best friends. We seemingly shared everything—from books, to pudding cups, to stuffed animals.

It made sense, then, that we would invite each other over. Lisa told me about the many toys she had, that she had a canopy bed, and that her father had built a dollhouse that was taller than her. I couldn't wait to go, but I had to first get permission from my mother, a strict first-generation Japanese woman who was very concerned about saving face. My mother spent two hours getting me ready for Lisa's house, with most of the time occupied on getting my hair just so. She repeatedly chastised me for not sitting still. She tightly grabbed my hair, repeatedly combing it to the point it hurt my scalp. My mother had carefully selected the "right" barrettes—sparkling accessories that stood out on fine, black hair. In hindsight, I think my mother knew. I don't know, but it seems like she did.

Lisa had planned an innocuous game of UNO (which, to this day, is a game I never play), followed by a dollhouse tour. I knocked on the door—not too loud, for my mother told me that you always have to be a perfect guest. A tall, skinny woman answered. In retrospect, she looked nothing like Lisa. With eyes narrowed and mouth creased, she hissed. I think she may have said she needed to talk with Lisa. She didn't slam the door so much as shut it. That was perhaps the kindest act she performed that day. Not knowing where to go, I sat on the steps, though I wished I had not. With no care of who sat discarded outside, Lisa's mother yelled at her daughter, stressing the myriad reasons why a "stinky gook" could not come indoors. Not only were gooks dirty; they were sneaky. They stole from a person's house. They ate smelly food. They wore clothes that reeked of mothballs. They were unclean for they never showered. They were "rats," and Lisa's mother did not want to let "rats" into her house.

The first time that you are asked, in uncomfortable often angry tones, to wait outside is a feeling you never forget. It's a feeling I still have—it sticks to the stomach, like a swallowed burr. The time you are involuntarily left outdoors, like discarded garbage, expands disproportionately to actual time. In those situations, you are asked to extend a politeness never imagined by the other person, to wait quietly perhaps, or—better yet—to walk back. Made to feel bad, silent, and different, you sit. And what you wait for is a chance to get back inside, to recapture what it means to be welcomed, friended, respected, and valued.

And, though that first time is memorable, what comes after is what haunts you. Word quickly spread, and by the day's end I was once again "left outdoors." As the rest of the school year made startling clear, "gooks" didn't have friends. They didn't deserve places in line, seats on a bus, nor a turn on the swing. They deserved, instead, to be left perpetually outside, and they don't ask to be let in. It is asking to be "let in" that I carry because of that seven-year-old memory.

Alvaro Saar Rios

Brown Enough

Dear Professor Mex-alot,
I write to you in dire need of your help.
According to your Mex-o-meter,
I'm not brown enough
because my music doesn't remind you of
the country my grandparents ran away from.
I'm not brown enough
because my skin and my clothes don't remind you of
the fields my parents grew up in.
I'm not brown enough
porque yo no hablo español.
I'm not brown enough
because I don't play into the media endorsed version of a true Mexican.
What do you want me to do?
Do you want me to wear GOODYEAR huaraches,
burlap jeans,
and a rope for a belt?
Do you want me to stop using my brain
and start renting out my back?
Do you want me to sweat on the weekdays,
drink on the weekends,
and have a wife who takes care of our 5, 4, 3, 2, 1 year old kids
and watches novelas
while cleaning our apartment with swollen hands and feet?
Do you want me to roll my r's and soften my ch's
when I'm speaking English?
How brown do you want me to be?
How brown do you want me to be?
Do you want me to write this letter a la charra
con cilantro y salsa
on a piece of cardboard or on the skin of maguey?
Do you want me to use a brown pen, too?
Should my breakfast consist of Beans & Rice Krispies

with jalapeño flavored marshmallows
and a tall healthy glass of Nopal flavored fruit juice?
Should I not employ an affirmative action program
when looking for a soul mate?
Should I forget the only language I know
just so I can learn the "true" brown experience?
I already know how it feels to be ignored and looked down upon.
Yo no hablo español, remember?
How brown do you want me to be?
How brown do you want me to be?
As your criticisms have soaked into the cuts you have created,
I've realized that the true brown experience
doesn't come from speaking Español—
the language of our conquerors.
It comes from Nahuatl—
the language that crumbled with our glorious pyramids.
And since you seem to have a Ph.D. in Mexology,
I want you to help me be a better brown person.
I need help translating a few words.
How do you say "kiss my ass?"
I do hope this letter finds you well.

Your amigo,

Edward Brownskin

Mary E. Delabruere

That Boy

That boy's chiseled face
cocked just at the right angle
some thirty years ago—
Flashy smile, cool shuffle
sent oooh warm waves shivering
from my spine to my mind.
Till leering my way
upper lip snarled at his prey—
eyes iced with disapproval—
slowly, subtly,
from side to side,
that head shook.
My jaw dropped—
a wordless "Why?"
Stripped of dignity,
of identity,
of authenticity
I crumbled like a dry cookie.
Ever since at a loss
to identify
to differentiate
beautiful and ugly.

Vanessa Otero

Addiction

For My Titi Loida

She can dance, dance, dance her ass off
In the Club
At the House
For fun, to feel free.
The music gets in her being, muscles, heart and mind
And she feels it through and through.
If she only had to dance
Life would be wonderful
But she needs to live in the real
Everyday
And it really is just too much.
The pain is the opposite of the music and when the music stops
She has to cope and medicate and numb.
Smoke some weed, snort some blow or manteca.
Do whatever it takes to cope and medicate and numb and heal.
Because the pain is the opposite of the music and when the music stops
She remembers the pain between her legs, his sweat falling on her face,
	his panting.
Every night she danced her ass off in the clubs.
The sound was beside her, in her.
Those moments on the dance floor seemed to help cope and medicate
	and heal.
That issue—her issue didn't exist.
But when the music stopped she remembered that the pain never
	stopped and
It had all gone too far.
That morning she remembered
Because she woke up with him
A different version of him,
Many versions of him over and over
And on the way back to Brooklyn on the train it sunk in.
The woman sitting next to her seemed to mind

That all of this was happening in front of her.
The nerve of a whore with years on her face and jeans way too tight to cry
And be a plain mess on the train.
She looked at the woman and laughed
For being half crazy and to ignite the disgust on the woman's face.
That night she danced, danced, danced her ass off at the club
And did what she does to cope, medicate, heal over and over and over
Sometimes in the shower or on the train back to Brooklyn it sinks in
And she decides to get better but it doesn't stick.
This is her life and sometimes getting out of it seems harder than
    staying in.

José B. Gonzalez

i couldn't for a teenaged bully's death

i couldn't for a teenaged bully's death
i couldn't for a bully's teen death—
shot in the abdomen three times—
trigger pulled by the hand of a child
who sought the bullet of a gun
to stop the bull's horns
from digging deeper into his abdomen.

before he died in the shadows of Victorians on Coit Street
he stole fieldstones from walls—only to crack them against storm doors—
& stored rocks in his yard so he could pack them with snow & whirl
them toward the heads of anyone who tried tiptoeing past his high rise—
the giant outline of his cradled body captured the enormity of his hands.

at 10 he used those hands to shove chests—
the beatings wouldn't rest against running backs—
even then he'd laugh as if chasing rabbits—
it was his habit to make the smaller ones cower.

by his 13th, teachers began crouching—
there was one who cried as he walked out of the principal's office—
it was as if he was offing them 1 by 1.

watching tv with the door locked—
that's where i was when i heard that his hands had been stopped—
on the news they showed people putting their hands over their mouths
as their lips trembled and they spoke about the times, the crimes.
but my fingers, they stayed tight like fists—
i couldn't for this bully's teen death—
not when this would end the thumping on chests—
i couldn't, though i wish my palms would at least rest—
wished his father's bars, his mother's scars,
hadn't turned him—me—us into this.

Lori Desrosiers

I Wanted To Be Wonder Woman

I wanted to be Wonder Woman,
red-lipped, curvaceous, strong.
Her lariat had the power
to make people tell the truth;
bullets bounced off her bracelets.

I would have used my lariat
on my mother
when she was going out,
and wouldn't tell me why;
to find out if her secret anger
was my fault.

I would have used it on my father
to make him tell why he left
so my mother could hear it.
Maybe they'd have talked it out.

I would have used it on my little brother,
make him tell how he always won at Monopoly,
and why he would be angry at me
for so many years in the future.

I wanted to be Wonder Woman
because she knew Superman,
and the Incredible Hulk,
friends who could scare off bullies,
like Debbie Finkel in fourth grade
who told me I would never be good enough
for her and her friends,
and I believed her.

Their mean words would have
bounced off my bracelets,
then I would have
put my lariat around their waists,
and make them tell the truth,
that I was a wonderful kid.

Judith Ortiz-Cofer

The Welcome Mat

On her 15th birthday, she walks out of the barrio in spite of her mother's warnings—ten blocks, past the stores named after saints and pueblos, the church with the sign of a Pentecostal service en español, and the bar with a door that is always half open, where the sign for go-go girls—a strobing blue nude—is on day and night, past the buildings with slush piled up to the curb, with muddy paths stomped out by those who must slog through to cross the street; past where almost everyone she knows lives—ten blocks to a different world. The doctor's daughter, who wrote an essay for Sister Olive's English class about the goodness-grace of having friends of all colors and persuasions, has given her directions to her house, where they will do homework together. It is Lent, and she suspects the doctor's daughter is using her as currency against her venial sins. Come over, we can celebrate your birthday. She will walk ten blocks beyond her gray world, walk until there is space and light, until the snow serves for decoration and play. A grinning-silly snowman in the yard. This section of town turns her into a wary-scary stranger, and she walks like one. The looks she gets from the cop watching over the neat houses and snow plowed streets, and from the postman delivering something fragile right into a woman's hands at her own door, tell her to walk with purpose, eyes forward. It has snowed and she is wearing the wrong shoes. Chinese slippers made of fake suede that lets everything she steps on seep in. Her feet are numb by the time she arrives at the house with the circular drive. She leaves wet footprints all the way to the front door. There she is asked by the worried-smiling woman to please take off her shoes at the welcome mat before she steps onto the white shag carpet. White shag from wall to wall. Please girls, eat your cupcakes in the kitchen! What she will remember of this day is how her shoes curl up as they dry in the sun, like black clams, like two curly-dead creatures left on the welcome mat by the dog, and how her friend stares in silence at her little brother, who lets out a whooping–mocking laugh-like sound when he sees her zapatos muertos. He whoops and jumps up and down once, before he covers his mouth and runs to the kitchen to share his dead shoes joke with his smiling-frowning mother.

Priscilla LaBoy

I Live in My Memories

to María Luisa, the first Hispanic female poet I have ever known

You can say that my body was raised in Springfield,
but my memories are still in New York City.
I slept between my mom and dad when I was a little girl,
not expecting that a place that is so comforting
with the people you love most
is the same place where I got to see my mom getting hurt.
Abuse—sad because of my dad.
I thought that by my mom moving to a new city,
the past was going to be the past,
and no one would get hurt.
But I was wrong and things just got worse.
I guess it was my turn.
Mom just had eyes for her new boyfriend.
I was just her bad memories
because all she sees is my father in me:
his big lips, light skin, and light brown eyes
she once loved. I don't even remember
when was the last time she gave me a hug.
Three years of loneliness and sadness go by.
Now I'm eleven years old and all my hopes and dreams
are gone because that is the year
that I just wanted my heart to stop. To stop
from beating because I didn't want to live anymore.
Why? Because instead of my mom
having her eyes on me,
someone else did and raped me.
I'm 28 years old now, and she don't know
till this day. I don't even know
if she would even care
that her happiness is and always will be
my nightmare.

Narelle Thomas

Natural Beauty

Why do you laugh when I'm myself
not that funny kind of laugh but . . .
the hurtful one
why do I go home feeling hurt
EVERY DAY
until pain overcomes my WHOLE body and tears through my brain
putting your words on display repeating and building
stronger each and every time
again and again until I almost believe your lies
why do I have to wear an elaborate disguise to hide
MYSELF and mask MY WORDS
with things that you'd like to hear
trying not to show my fear of being hurt and put down another day
I go to school and ask what will it be TODAY?
my kinky hair
or my old hat to cover it?
will it be my lips or the way that I suck them in
to try to make them look like that supermodel on tv?
is it the shoes that i didn't buy yesterday
or the day before
that makes you call me poor
is it that i don't pronounce my words as clearly as you do
or how my family DOESN'T have enough money
to supply me with whatever stuff i wish for?
so i go home
and ask my mom a different question every day
why can't i have a relaxer or a flat iron at least?
why is my nose wide and my lips big
with cheek bones that reach for the sky?
why can't I at least have ONE more pair of shoes
or show jewelry like the other kids
so one day she sat me down and i thought
oh no i've ALREADY said TOO MUCH

she knows EVERYTHING i'm thinking
and then she told me that that's what makes me different
that i'm the way that I'm SUPPOSED to be
a NATURAL beauty
that I don't need to wear a mask to it and be like everyone else
I can be myself
me
I don't need to wear a hat to cover my hair
my kinks and curls are beautiful and my features are lively
she told me that I should NEVER have shame for being myself
and should use my words to make them think
show them how to love themselves too
and how we can ALL help each other
and learn to LOVE each other so much
that we can push our differences aside
and sew our similarities together
and just be us
the MANY that form ONE

Eilish Thompson

On Cyber Faux Power: An Essay with an Attitude

If you don't have the guts required to spit a cruel name into someone's visage when they're standing face to face with you, send them a myspace threat. Or text them with an unequivocally detestable message worded as to insult them completely with fabricated truths to assure them that no good thing, or anything worthy of praising, exists in them. Or let them in on the secret that their flaw, usually limited to the price tag on their shirt, overpowers their qualities. Let them fester in this truth which explains, somehow, why they fall into that seventy-seven percentile range of all school children. The percentage everyone laughs at. Do this in the name of cyber power simply because they are indisputably subservient to you and your virtues. But whatever you do, do not let yourself get caught up in their emotions. Do not allow yourself to see the tears form in their wounded eyes. And most importantly, do not ever take a step back to look at it from their perspective.

The technologically savvy bully must always begin their career in chat rooms. Hidden from a guardian's influence, one must surf the web on a board composed of insults. Blocked from fists and tears by the computer screen, the cyber bully must intimidate the kids who wish they could fit in. This is the how one gets power in the bullying world: intimidation. After all, to be able to be afraid of nothing but your hideous and uncaring heart is a powerful thing. Real bullies aspire to own such a heart if only because it cannot feel and therefore does not understand what it is putting others through.

Then the cyber bully must familiarize themselves with myspace and facebook. These two tools will prove immensely helpful, especially if one can get the victim's email and password. Once one has attained these things, one can begin to hack their myspace or facebook and post nasty comments or photoshopped pictures aimed to embarrass them.

In order to truly exacerbate the issue to the point of no morale-return for one's victim, take pictures of them changing in the locker room and post them on myspace or facebook. One can even do it anonymously to ensure one's personal identity is not revealed. It always works.

Sometimes, if a cyber bully is lucky and cruel enough to be effective, the victim will respond in ways that are traumatizing to the average soul. Take for example, Phoebe Prince of South Hadley High School. If you, the cyber bully, cannot take the idea of some Irish transfer dating the boy that you just have to have, then text her with malicious terms. Allow jealousy to fill that void that any cyber bully must possess, instead of kindness and acceptance. If she responds to your cyber actions with extreme depression and suicidal thoughts, then you have achieved your ultimate goal. If your victim, led by you to the cliff, takes the final step off, then you, being the cyber bully, have done something awesome. That is: something so overwhelming which will have a tremendous effect of fear rippling through every person you know when they figure out that you are the infamous cyber bully.

Actions taken by cyber bullies against victims can be so destructive that they are devastating to any normal person. But it must be understood that bullies are in fact not normal people. They have an abnormal need to feel power. They do everything and anything to get that power. And if something horrible happens as a result of their quest for power, they brush it off with the chip in their shoulder. They never see anything as their fault. But how could they? How can one see anything if one's eyes are only focusing on one thing? Especially if that one thing is the need for power. Power-hungry people are one of the worst types of people to come across, or to strike as a potential target. A potential refilling station, if you will.

Cyber bullying is a significant issue in modern life. It is imperative that change be sought. Its effects are extremely potent; the victim drowns themselves in the negative feelings towards them that it provokes, and the bully becomes addicted towards the strong sense of power it produces. As long as there is easy access to computers, websites, and technology in general, cyber bullying will always cause trouble. However, it is the actions we can take to prevent it that are necessary. It is the support we can give to both the victims and the bullies that is needed. Everyone needs to have their flame of power ignited, but it needs to be done by striking the match of acceptance, caring and friendship in each other. Friendships provide a power that is a hundred-fold better and healthier for the world than enemies.

RESOLUTION

"Although the world is full of suffering, it is also full
of the overcoming of it."
—Helen Keller

Sam Plotkin

Walking this Path

Fighting in an army
That consists of only me
But I have to move on
Nobody will understand
Nobody in all the land
Yet I still remain strong

I wonder what my future holds
I wonder if my heart will unfold

Chorus:
But one thing I know
Is I have strength by myself
No one can take my hope
Its my greatest wealth
Its been far too long walking this path alone
Like I'm out in the wilderness on my own

I have nothing left to lose
These broken pieces I will use
To build my hope again
Sometimes it seems that people don't care
But I realize I'm not stuck anywhere
And I will make it
don't know how, when or where

I wonder what my future holds
I wonder if my heart will unfold

Chorus:
But one thing I know
Is I have strength by myself
No one can take my hope
It's my greatest wealth
It's been far too long walking this path alone
Like I'm out in the wilderness on my own

Iris Morales

The Power of Direct Action

The men in my family had very strict views about gender roles. Men controlled the household and made all decisions even though their wives were strong and had jobs outside the home. Girls were at the bottom of the hierarchy and were referred to as "chancletas"—disposable slippers. Men like my father, who had only daughters and no sons, were ridiculed for being "chancleteros" or "slipper producers." Others would mock my father for having four daughters; he would squirm with embarrassment. I watched him, feeling demeaned and angry that he did not speak up for us "chancletas." I wanted to speak but did not yet know exactly why it bothered me so, and what I should say. The men in my family would speak to their wives referring to me, "Her responsibility is to get married, to be a good wife and have children." I would get angry when I heard this; but it was just assumed that I would comply. My mother, godmother and aunts were the messengers. They worried about me. I came to hate any sentence that began, "To be a good wife, you must . . . learn to cook. To be a good wife, you must . . . fill the tub for your husband in the evening. To be a good wife, you must . . . fetch his slippers. I rebelled against the expectation that I would center my life around serving a husband and having children. I declared to the family, "I will not do any of those things. Are men invalids? He can cook and fetch his own things," I said. For my opinions, I was branded, "rebelde" or rebel, and "machúa," which means like a man. My cousins were forbidden to hang out with me.

In school, I faced more barriers in the form of racism that questioned my intelligence and attempted to break my spirit. When I approached Miss B., the guidance counselor, about helping me apply to college, she informed me, in a serious and seemingly caring tone, "Unfortunately, you are not college material." I was shocked; I had worked hard since middle school when I had been truant and in trouble. I had turned around in high school, earned good grades, was elected student government vice president, and had a role in the school play. But Miss B. insisted. "You'll never make it into a four-year college," she explained. At the time, the prestigious city university system of New York City offered free tuition, and each college required a high grade point average for admission. The mainly all white institution—students, faculty, and administration—had only a few students of color at the four-year universities—about 1.5 percent of the total enrollment according to public records. People of color were there as kitchen and janitorial employees. But, I had it in my head that I wanted to attend a four-year university. I was so angry with Miss B. for discouraging me that I cursed her over and over, and wished her dead. Against her instructions, I applied to the City College of New York anyway as an evening, non-matriculated student. A couple of weeks later, she died suddenly of a heart attack. As karma would have it, Susan, the student government president, called me and said that we had to speak at Miss B.'s memorial service to express our grief on behalf of the student body. We went; we spoke, but I don't remember what we said. I know that we felt guilty. We had both cursed her on more than one occasion and wished her dead.

Immediately after high school graduation, I took a job at the West Side Block Association as a tenant organizer. Working out of a storefront office, I spent my days in the neighborhood knocking door-to-door, speaking with tenants about their housing conditions, organizing meetings, filling out legal forms, making court appearances and serving as an English/Spanish language translator. Several evenings a week, the tenant association met to plan actions against greedy landlords and corrupt city building inspectors and to coordinate rent strikes. I loved organizing and became known around the neighborhood. Over and over, I witnessed injustices and racism, and how the legal system was stacked against the poor.

In one case, I went to court several times with Mrs. Pérez trying to compel the landlord to deal with the rat infestation in the building where she lived. The first judge chastised us saying, "You can't just waltz willy-nilly into this court claiming that there are rats in a building. The law requires proof, and, I don't know how it's done in whatever country you come from, but, here, in America, you have to bring evidence of your claim." So I asked, "How do we prove rat infestation?" Kiddingly, I added, "Should we bring the rats to court?" "No, just the rat droppings," he responded seriously. I couldn't believe it; I was outraged, but we went back to Mrs. Pérez's apartment, collected rat droppings and took them to court. When we appeared before the second judge, he said, "Now how does the court know that the droppings are from the apartment that you claim? You could have collected the droppings from a construction site or any other place," he said. In my mind, I thought, "What a small man. Does he believe that we have nothing better to do with our lives than gather rat shit?" Out loud, I asked, "So how do we prove that the droppings are from Mrs. Pérez's apartment?" "Bring in pictures," he said. "I'm sure you can find someone who has a camera and speaks English," he said. The next time, the judge said that pictures were not good evidence because they could be doctored. We went back and forth with the housing court in this ridiculous and disdainful way, and in the end, the legal system did nothing.

One morning, Mrs. Pérez called me screaming hysterically that she woke up to find a huge rat crawling into her newborn baby's crib. Screeching at the top of her lungs, "I'm going to kill him! The landlord! I'm going to kill him!" Believing her, I rushed to her apartment. When the landlord arrived a little later, I told him that his life was in peril. "Mrs. Pérez is going to kill you," I said. He immediately ordered the super to stuff poison and steel wool wire into the gaping rat holes and even replaced all of Mrs. Pérez's kitchen appliances with new ones. That day I wondered whether the legal system was pure evil or just impotent, but in any case, I learned the power of direct action.

Later that summer, I received a letter from City College of New York informing me that I was accepted. Miss B. must be turning in her grave, I thought.

Teatro V!da Youth Ensemble

In Living Memory

Carl Joseph Walker-Hoover
Mario Hornsby, Jr.
Phoebe Prince
Conor Reynolds
Sowayne Wayne Rankin
Brittany Pérez
Corey Melvin
Nicholas Hiller

Those we have known.
Those we will never know.

We honor your memory.
We celebrate your lives.
To our community we say:
No dejes que la violencia entre en tu vida.
íResiste!
Con la vida no se juega,
no dejes que el fantasma de la violencia
te haga un lío en la cabeza.
íResiste!
We demand an end to violence.
íResiste!
We have lost so many. Loved ones. Friends. Peers.
Praise the life they lived. Young, full of opportunity.
Don't let the violence take over.

To our community we say: Stand up to violence!
íResiste!
Don't let fear take over.

Open your mind, leave it clear. In this moment, remember.

I will always remember that beautiful smile when you were telling me
    your dreams.

Bring love, peace, joy. Relate. Remember those who have passed away.

I will always remember that beautiful smile when you were telling me
    your dreams.

We will honor, celebrate your lives, by sharing parts of ourselves
    with others.
We will honor your lives by accepting others for who they are.

We will honor your lives by being ourselves.
Together we can build up our community.

Praise the life they lived. Young, full of opportunity.

Shed the hate in your eyes, so that we may smile again.

I will always remember that beautiful smile when you were telling me
    your dreams:

Carl Joseph Walker-Hoover
Mario Hornsby, Jr.
Conor Reynolds
Sowayne Wayne Rankin
Brittany Pérez
Corey Melvin
Nicholas Hiller
Those we have known.
Those we will never know.

We will honor your life by being ourselves.
Together we can build up our community.

For all who have suffered pain that others have caused.
We remember you. We will honor your life by accepting others for who
    they are.

We will honor your life by being ourselves. Together we can stop violence
    in your memory.
We miss you. We love you. We respect you. We honor you.
We demand courage. We stand against violence.

Do something, but give your heart to it.

There are messages that are supposed to help, but don't have passion.

You hurt others by not taking action.
Do something, but give your heart to it.

No dejes que el fantasma de la violencia
te haga un lío en la cabeza.
íResiste!
We walk without looking around.
We speak, but don't know how.

Wake up! This is an important matter!

Do something, but give your heart to it.
Make a change:
In your home. In your school. In your heart. On the street.

Don't gang up on each other, gang up on the issue.
Take a stand, demand . . . an end to violence.
íResiste!

Carl Joseph Walker-Hoover
Mario Hornsby, Jr.
Phoebe Prince
Conor Reynolds
Sowayne Wayne Rankin
Brittany Pérez
Corey Melvin
Nicholas Hiller

Those we have known. Those we will never know. We honor your memory. We celebrate your lives.

We will always remember that beautiful smile as you still tell us your dreams.

Narelle Thomas

Liberation

I am a butterfly in a jar waiting to be freed
self-expression is key to my being
lending a helping hand and a listening ear are
my expertise
I search for light in the darkest places in truths within
this heap of lies
I walk the tightrope of life guided by honesty, hope,
love and aspiration
my heart shows me what my eyes can't
thinking freely with creativity is important to me
but school and other places try and narrow my way of
thinking
limiting it to inside of the box instead of where it wants
to be
self-expression is strong and naturally occurring and
allows me to escape the jar and once again become
free

Emmy Cepeda
Vecinas

Lo percibo en el aire
Por la ropa que compro
Por la comida que como
Lo escucho venir
Oigo sus pasos
A mi se acercan los murmullos

Añorando mi mirada
Lo siento
Sus ojos en mi espalda
Esperando mi primer tropiezo
Para penetrar mi piel
Con alargadas pezuñas
Para devorarme paso a paso
Con sus infamias

Puedo escuchar los murmullos
El viento los carga y llega a mis oídos
Los comentarios negativos
Soy la comedia de todos
La envidia que los motiva

¿Sabes qué? Los bochinches
Son música a mis oídos

Me entristece como la gente
Pierde el tiempo en negativismo
Como desperdician sus vidas
Viviendo las vidas de otro.

No me importa lo que digan
Yo sigo siendo quien soy
No me detengo ante la baratija
De quien soy yo Segura estoy

Emmy Cepeda

Neighbors
(translation by María Luisa Arroyo)

I sense it in the air
Because of the clothes I buy
Because of the food I eat
I hear it coming
I hear its steps
The murmuring gets closer to me

Missing my gaze
I feel it
Their eyes in my back
Waiting for my first falter
In order to penetrate my skin
With elongated claws
To devour me bit by bit
With their infamy

I can hear the murmurs
The wind carries them and they reach my ears
The negative comments
I am everyone's laughingstock
Envy motivates them

You know what? Gossip
Is music to my ears

It saddens me how people
Waste time in negativity
How they waste their lives
Living the lives of others.

I don't care what they say
I will continue to be who I am
I don't let their trifling stop me
I am Sure of who I am

Shel Horowitz

How Being Bullied Led to My Empowerment

As a child, I was bullied a lot. Growing up in the Bronx, I was small, weak, and didn't play sports. And worse, I was always reading . . . voluntarily. So I was a pretty easy target.

One day when I was about eleven, one of the local thug-punks, a kid about my age with a big swastika on his jacket, cornered me on the street and started waving a length of chain in my face, threatening to beat me with it.

And a little old lady who lived in my building stalked up to him and told him loudly and firmly to leave me alone! She was probably in her sixties or seventies, and not over five feet tall—but she wasn't going to let this creep go around intimidating people. He left—and I realized that we ordinary folk actually did have power, that I didn't have to accept being bullied, and that I didn't have to accept injustice. I could even put some wrongs to right.

That insight was one of the forces that moved me toward a lifetime of making the world better in whatever ways I can. I've put many decades into social justice and environmental work, and I can point to several instances where I've made an impact, including starting a movement that saved our much-loved local mountain from a particularly nasty luxury home development. When the story announcing the project was published, the reporter quoted a number of people in the environmental community with variations on "this is terrible, but there's nothing we can do!" But that neighbor had shown me thirty years earlier that they were wrong, that we could do something. The first meeting of Save the Mountain was held in my dining room two weeks later, and we went on to involve thousands of people, and protect the mountain permanently in just thirteen months (I'd expected it would take five years).

Following that success, I launched a ten-year, world-wide movement to promote business ethics, at www.business-ethics-pledge.org. This campaign has moved very slowly, but I do feel it's beginning to help change the culture of greed and domination that's all-too-common in the business world. And at least I didn't say—and I will never say—"this is terrible, but there's nothing we can do!"

Susan Hucul

Choices

As we traverse the many roads that are part of teaching and working with students, we are often confronted with situations that are difficult to navigate. Bullying, in particular, has become one of the unfortunate realities of our journey. Although bullying has always existed in one form or another, the degree to which it has grown has become a great sadness to parents, educators and the students. I have witnessed many forms, but for the first time, this year, I was part of a situation that was baffling.

I have always prided myself on my ability to diffuse situations in which one student was made to feel lesser than one of their peers, but a situation presented itself this year that left me feeling quite clueless. I often wonder about what leads one to the decision that it is o.k. to make another feel badly, often doing more damage than they realize. This year, one group of girls, in particular, quickly became my focus as I witnessed them behaving like tight-knit family members one minute, then arch enemies the next. All of them began taking part in behaviors that would begin with mild teasing then culminate into serious mental abuse. Five teachers, including myself, brought them together to talk about what was happening to try and figure out a solution.

Narelle Thomas

Soaring Upward

Sometimes i sit and wonder what it feels like to be a bird . . . to be free
to fly in the sky . . . and soar . . . up
so high . . . above everything
making it seem so small
with great distance . . . higher and higher
confident . . . not worried about falling
birds seem so small to people but birds are like us . . . there are many of
    both of us
but they sing to each other
they have nests
they even build from the environment . . . communities
they have a . . . togetherness
they speak to each other . . . without shame of themselves
they sing out loud for everyone to hear
they speak their languages
the many pitches tones and caws
and each are understood commonly
with no flaw . . . they are free
they don't need tv to show them reality
they are free
to fly must mean to have no limits . . . no boundaries . . . no animosity . . .
togetherness
being happy with yourself and others
being true and in tune with the things around you
and if people are so much like birds . . . what happened?
where did we go wrong?
birds live with each other cooperatively
they don't judge like we do
some say that they like to be firmly planted to the ground but i ask . . .
    why? . . . we aren't
trees
but even trees look to their roots for guidance
birds have each other to lean on . . . they understand

they fly together
they don't have to change "to fit" in because they know that they
    naturally belong
where did we go wrong?
they aren't confined . . . with trapped minds . . .
we like having our minds in the clouds . . . afraid to come down
we seem to be so tied back and down by the temporary chains of earth
if only we could see through the eyes of the birds
they can fly through the trees . . . past the clouds
and never look down, for the fall but instead look
towards the sun
why can't we fly? . . . i wonder
sometimes i sit and watch the birds and become inspired
as i continue to look . . . i dream
i see us and them too
flying with wings of infinity . . . higher
higher
and . . .
higher

Sam Plotkin
(written at at age thirteen)

Don't Stop Living

You make your way through life
wondering if you're good for anyone
You can't keep up with all the pain stored in your mind
The journey you walk is taking long
But you will never stop playing your song
When people try to bring you down
Just lift your head up high and don't make a sound

Run for your life
and don't stop running
breath for your life and don't stop breathing
look deep inside and it won't take long 'till you find your way
Give all you have and don't stop giving
Look for a dream that keeps you driven
Live for your life cause you'll never get it back if you throw away
Don't stop living your life
Everyday

Be open minded to the people that come your way
Give them a chance and hear what they have to say
And if they don't do the same
You are not the one to blame
There's different ways to play the game
Just shoot for what you want with a steady aim

Run for your life
and don't stop running
breath for your life and don't stop breathing
look deep inside and it won't take long 'till you find your way

Give all you have and don't stop giving
Look for a dream that keeps you driven
Live for your life cause you'll never get it back if you throw away
Don't stop living your life
Everyday

Evan Plotkin

My Son Was Bullied

My son Sam was bullied in middle school. Often kids would not let him sit next to them on the bus. He was teased and came home in tears.

As parents this was an extremely difficult time. Sam's focus in life has been, and continues to be, around music and song writing. Often it is the creative kids who don't play sports that get bullied. Sam expressed his situation at the time in a song he wrote that appeared on his first CD *Stepping Out* called "What Leads to Happiness."

It goes something like this, to a reggae beat: "When you are having a sitting alone on the bus kind of day, and nothing seems to be going your way . . . I sing . . . and I jump into a new world and leave my past behind . . ."

It was a true expression of his spirit and how in his own way through music he overcame his fears. Sam is now a very gifted singer and song-writer.

Great art is often created when the inner self is trying to overcome great physical or emotional stresses.

Sam's story has a happy ending. But we know that they don't all end this way.

Narelle Thomas

Power: A Struggle

power, a struggle
power . . . what you crave more than happiness
power that you work to receive
power that's not in the money . . . but you know that . . .
and you still try to bury into my brain
that you have more and spend so much of it on me
power that is not gained from slapping me in the face
because i speak words that contain it
the respect in my eyes that you lose
you can not break me
i give you respect that only grows . . .
until you disrespect me, thinking that violence
or confrontational behavior gives power to you
you speak words that should make me feel low but they don't
negativity doesn't bring my power down
power is deeply rooted within me
with soil full of mer hotep and ma'at*
which give power
to absorb nourishment from the life i eat
that positivity . . . you can't take from me
i know that you have power too . . .
you just have to find it and let it grow
before you try to use it so it will thrive with respect
and that negativity will be no where to be found
you can give yourself respect and learn
to believe in yourself because you carry power
you are strong and have brought lives
full of light into this world
don't let yours burn out
and don't give up yet because you deserve more
you deserve love peace harmony truth and respect

*Ancient Egyptian words meaning: light (mer), to be at peace (hotep), and principle of divine truth (ma'at).

you are strong and beautiful
your power will fully bloom and shine
you can be that flower
you have that foundational soil
you have power

Judge William H. Abrashkin

So That the Children Will Be Saved

Why is it that they think, or act as if they think,
That precepts of the world:
    Cause and effect,
    Thoughtfulness,
    Morality against self-interest,
Like flags, must be unfurled and waved
so that the children will be saved?

Each childish day transfigured to morality play.
The principles will not shrink, or even start to shrink away.
They need not be flung
    Like stones,
    Like darts,
    Like words.
Better bite the tongue, and know
that minds and hearts will grow.

But no. The thoughts with roots in deep-held fears
admonish now the youthful years.
    They can't.
    They won't.
    I can't I won't.
And laying words like bricks, they almost can believe
that they themselves are wise, and peace of mind retrieve.

Nenah Sylver

In Search of the Real Man / Real Woman

"You walk like a soldier." My mother's indictment startled me, and the sneer on her lips smarted. My arms were only swinging the way they are supposed to when you walk with determined steps. But this was just before the second wave of the Women's Liberation movement, when women were expected to be "dainty" and "ladylike"—in other words, refrain from indulging in rigorous, free movements. Women were also supposed to look a certain way, and Mom tried her best to indoctrinate me with her dress code. But rouge made me itch, high-heeled shoes threw me off-balance, and girdles were so tight I could barely breathe. So she and I fought, constantly.

Mom subscribed to some mighty strange notions. She'd been brought up to believe that if she did not look or behave in certain ways, she was not a Real Woman. Dad, on the other hand, was exempt from her dress code. He was allowed to "walk like a soldier." And he was allowed (and encouraged) to engage in activities forbidden to my mother—all part of his appointed role as a Real Man.

As I would discover from a young age, there were countless unwritten laws dictating how Real Women and Real Men should act. Whenever I saw my mother indulge in elaborate machinations to pretend she wasn't intelligent—because, according to her, my father's ego should be boosted since he was the man—I learned that she was being a Real Woman. Whenever I heard my father yell at my mother when dinner was five minutes late—because, according to him, she should service him on demand since she was the woman—I learned that he was being a Real Man. And whenever my sister cried because my brother, who was trying to be a Real Man, beat her up, I learned that she was being a Real Woman.

An unlimited supply of rules and regulations existed outside my family, too. They were enforced even in kindergarten, where the boys were assigned to play with electric trains and the girls (who were prohibited from crossing over to the boys' side) were allowed only to putter with miniature kitchen sets. Since by that time I was cooking my own breakfast, I didn't see why duplicating at school the work I had to do at home was considered "fun." It was a war I couldn't win, making me resentful and sullen.

After weeks of futilely eyeing the trains, I again turned my back on the tiny stoves and pots and slipped into the magic world of books, teaching myself to read bigger words.

But those books I read as a child never explained to my satisfaction why I mustn't play with electric trains. Why were there such disparate principles guiding the behavior of men and women, boys and girls? What was a Real Man, anyway? And precisely what was a Real Woman? Considering all the hoopla required to launch me into my womanhood, my possessing female genitalia apparently wasn't enough to qualify me as a Real Woman. There were other things I needed to embrace, do and become.

I failed miserably. In those turbulent sixties, I was accused of embodying qualities that offended not only the existing norms, but also those who accused me of defecting. At various times, my adversaries charged that: I looked like a boy (when I kissed another girl); looked like a girl (when I was developing breasts); thought too rationally, like a boy (my father even nicknamed me Univac, after the first computer); and was too emotional, like a girl (I cried because people picked on me). Incredibly, at some point I was even called a faggot—which confused more than hurt me. Undoubtedly my tormenters were grasping at the first available insult.

Bottom line, the crime I'd committed that made me the lowest of the low, sub-human even, was my inability to be classified. Yet even a cursory examination of all the accusations I'd accrued revealed something seriously flawed with the reasoning behind the charges. How could I be criticized one moment for behaving too much like a male, and then the next moment be criticized for behaving too much like a female—which I thought I was supposed to act like anyway?

My confusion mounted. Not surprisingly, by the time I reached my teens, cataloging people's similarities and differences had become my passion. I resolved to unearth everything I could about what made a man Real and what made a woman Real.

Classifying people into the "Man" or "Woman" category proved more difficult than it looked. For instance, I kept forgetting that women weren't supposed to speak up, because my mother felt free to criticize me—loudly—anytime and anywhere. And it slipped my mind that men weren't supposed to engage in domestic activities, because my favorite uncle—who owned a large company and traveled all over the world for his business—was a superb knitter, and gave me lessons.

My cataloguing system really fell apart when I became romantically involved with a woman during my second year of college. Since "Man" and "Woman" were defined partly by the sex of their romantic partners, what did that make me? Was I the Real Woman? Or was my partner the Real Woman? Furthermore, if amorous relationships were defined as existing between a (Real) man and a (Real) woman, what did that make us? Or our relationship?

The label "lesbian" was problematic. It seemed reasonable enough to call me a lesbian when I related sexually to women. But what about the times I chose men as lovers? Then, the world perceived me as heterosexual. But did this mean that I was only half of a Real Woman? Or did it mean that I was a Real Woman, half the time?

Which led to another quandary. Even when I had a (as far as I knew, Real) man as my lover, it did not guarantee my Real Womanhood. I remembered during high school, when the mother of a nice senior boy I was dating warned him of rumors that I was on drugs (which wasn't true), and that I was a lesbian (which wasn't true—yet—either). I felt amused by the first allegation and complimented by the second. Was I thus accused because I had admittedly offbeat ideas, and lesbians were also considered offbeat? But they were also different because they obviously didn't care, as much as their straight counterparts did, about dressing or behaving in ways to please men. Put another way, they had some independence and spunk. So why did so many people snicker "lesbian" as though it were an offense?

Fortunately, my long-ago high school lover didn't listen to his mother. He didn't care whether he was kissing a heterosexual, a lesbian, or a kangaroo, for that matter. We liked and respected and enjoyed each other, and that was good enough for him. But that relationship further impressed upon me how language can be used as a weapon.

There were many ways to hurt with words. Athletic girls were admiringly called "tomboys" because they were coordinated and strong and behaved the way boys were supposed to, while gentle and klutzy boys were ridiculed as "sissies" because presumably they were like girls. Years later, a seminal journal article would confirm that males were indeed much more highly regarded than females. Respondents to a psychological survey equated maleness with self-reliance and strength (qualities of being an adult), and femaleness with dependence and helplessness (qualities ascribed to children). I remember how depressed I felt when that study came out. If I grew up to become a Real Woman, was I destined to remain a child?

My parents valued education above all else, so there was no question that after high school I'd go to college. I looked forward to continuing my Important Exploration in a scholastic environment. Surely I could learn how to be a Real Woman at a university, whose professors had undoubtedly spent years perfecting the art of Real Womanhood and Real Manhood.

My first foray into higher education was at a private old New England college, rich in history and tradition. But the books I was assigned to read (called "classics") only compounded my bewilderment. I read about wives who were beaten and harangued by their husbands. But because they did the right thing by pretending that they enjoyed this arrangement, and denied having any needs or aspirations, they were praised—as Real Women. One famous story, set in 17th century Puritan Boston, depicted a woman who had a child out of wedlock and was ridiculed. I didn't see any advantage to her situation, either.

Perhaps I could find better role models of Real Womanhood outside 17th, 18th and 19th century classical literature. So the following year I enrolled at a larger, more liberal university with a promising women's studies department. There, I was assigned radically different reading material. One outstanding work was the biography of Victoria Woodhull—publisher, sexual freedom advocate and investor—who not only scandalized the world with her numerous (unmarried) love affairs, but also made a fortune on the stock exchange. However, there seemed to be a question about whether Woodhull was a Real Women. Mom certainly didn't think she was.

By now, the exhilarating energy of Gay Liberation as well as Women's Liberation had infused universities across the country, and radical activists of all stripes were flocking to my school like locusts to a wheat field. This gave me hope. Getting involved with Lesbian Liberation would surely broaden my perspective, so I began attending meetings.

At first those meetings were encouraging. Among the lesbians, I met vibrant, strong women who related to each other as friends and lovers all rolled into one. Had I finally found my niche? But I began noticing a disconcerting dress code within the lesbian community. Many women wore plaid flannel shirts and short hair, viewing with disdain their stereotypically feminine lesbian sisters who wore high heels, tight skirts, heady perfume and bright lipstick. I myself detested anything that hindered my movement, clogged my sinuses or stained my clothes; but I did not have a large selection of flannel shirts in my wardrobe, either. Into what category of lesbian did my manner of dress consign me? For a brief time, my Important Exploration was sidetracked, and instead of searching for a Real Woman, I focused on finding a Real Lesbian.

As it turned out, flannel shirts were just the tip of the iceberg. They seemed to epitomize the much-publicized "butch-femme" relationships I'd heard so much about, and now realized were widely practiced. The "butch" persona was modeled after a Real Man, and the "femme" persona was modeled after a Real Woman. I couldn't wrap my mind around this. If both people in a lesbian relationship were female, how could the "butch" be a Real Man? And since both members of the couple were female, could even the "femme" be a Real Woman?

Which led me to another quandary. What was the advantage to being a lesbian if you ended up getting stuck with the same old Real Man/Real Woman script?

Despite my doubts about Lesbian Liberation, I kept going to meetings. But I achieved little clarity and obtained no relief. Many of the lesbians I met were soon exploring their Real Womanhood. What our culture called feminine, they insisted, was powerful and positive—and although gentleness and receptivity were not culturally valued, those traits were in fact more desirable than so-called male traits. I wrestled with this, ashamed of myself for still preferring certain "male" characteristics. Being feminine was so—well, wimpy. Who wanted to be a doormat (albeit a lovely and gracious one), if being that way wasn't respected, and only invited everyone to walk all over you?

It was the cruelest of ironies. Here I was, surrounded by attractive, warm women, a number of whom I wanted to know intimately—who were so appealing partly because their primary goal was to become the quintessential Earth Mother!

My world was rearranging itself at a dizzying pace. Across the nation, lesbians were buying houses and having children together via artificial insemination. My feminist friends (including myself) were growing their hair long again and looking suspiciously more and more like Real Women.

It was only a matter of time until bisexuals would form their own movement. When they did, giant buttons with the motto "Bi Is Beautiful" were displayed everywhere—in conference rooms, at conventions, during Pride parades. Was there a place for me with these people, free of rules and regulations on how to look and behave?

Alas, it was a mixed bag. Even within Bi Liberation, a surprisingly large number of women behaved like spineless sex kittens, and too many men acted like macho cavemen. I supposed this was to be expected—after all, movements are comprised of people from all walks of life. Yet in all the Bi Lib groups I visited, from San Francisco to New York to London, I kept hearing bisexuals express how unbalanced they felt relating sexually to only women, or only men. They needed both women and men in their lives to feel complete. In a movement of activists who presumably didn't want to be limited by the criteria of Real Womanhood or Real Manhood, here was an implicit admission of essential differences between men and women. And they weren't talking about genitalia.

Maybe more subtle differences did exist—after all, didn't I sometimes crave a night out with just "the girls?" And, as much as I disliked admitting it, sometimes I'd notice that a man had very "female" energy, or a woman seemed to be more "male." It was hard to dismiss this entirely as a matter of conditioning. But which came first—the energy, or the behavior that then changes the person's energy? No one I questioned, not even several prominent feminists, knew the answer. The most enlightening exchange came from a teacher who said that if I really wanted to learn about energy, I should go to graduate school and get a doctorate in quantum physics.

By now, transvestites (mostly males, called "cross-dressers") were showing up at the newly-named Gay, Lesbian and Bisexual Liberation meetings. Apparently, wearing glittery dresses and tons of mascara also meant walking with careful steps and vocalizing as a soprano. These people did not attempt to hide that they were neither Real Men nor Real Women. Yet why were they considered to be "in drag," whereas heavily made-up, breathy-voiced women in push-up bras and two-inch high heels, were not? How could clothing on one class of people be considered a costume at best and an aberration at worst, while on another class of people that same clothing was regarded as ordinary attire?

Then out-of-the-closet transsexuals began joining the get-togethers, demanding that the name "Transsexual" be added to "Gay, Lesbian and

Bisexual Liberation," and clamoring for their own spot in the sexual liberation parades.

Frustrated, I withdrew from all this liberation. It got terribly boring discussing sex and sexual orientation all the time, anyway; and whatever my sexuality was, I wanted it to simply be a part of life, the scenery along the path up the mountain rather than the mountain itself. If ever the time was that I needed a break, this was it.

Yet I was driven; I still had not found the Real Man or the Real Woman. At this point, my Important Exploration escalated into an All-Encompassing Quest. This required my transfer to yet another university (now in New York City), where I changed my major for a third time. If I really wanted to find Answers, I should study psychology in depth, with people who Knew. In a syllabus of my own design, I read voraciously: about different cultures in Africa, women and child care in China, the suffragist movement in the United States, and of course sexual behavior. Surely learning to master the mysteries of the human psyche—and with access to one of the largest libraries in the world—I would finally unearth what it meant to be a Real Woman, what it meant to be a Real Man.

What I found instead were enthralling facts that only sparked more questions. Some African tribes reversed roles. At first glance that seemed terrific, but, wait a minute—men who acted as women do in our culture, and women who acted like men? This meant there were circumscribed rules to follow. What was the use of role reversal as long as there were still roles to reverse? Why couldn't people simply act any way they chose?

If my genitals alone did not hold the answer to my Realness, maybe being a Real Woman or Real Man was associated with the more subtle biochemistry and genetics that had created those genitals. So I took up fetal biology. What wondrous tidbits I gleaned!

The popular story of females having XX chromosomes and males having XY chromosomes wrapped the sexes into nice neat packages. The problem was, these categories were fictional. Rather than the two archetypal paths—one leading to Real Womanhood and the other leading to Real Manhood—there were many different forks in the road down which the developing fetus can travel, all with different outcomes. You could get: females with internalized male organs due to what was considered a birth defect; women with an "overabundance" of testosterone that conferred muscular strength greater than the average female; and the extremely rare case of males possessing XX chromosome patterns. Sometimes people were diagnosed as hermaphrodites, possessing an XX chromosome pattern and born with both male and female internal organs. On other occasions, children were born not only with the male XY pattern and testes, but also an impaired ability to either produce or respond to testosterone—making them sometimes appear as "defective" females.

In practical terms, these deviations away from Real Manhood and Real Womanhood meant counseling for the parents, to help them decide which sex to enforce on their child—accompanied by the requisite surgical "correction" of the offspring's genitalia, along with treatment during puberty with the corresponding hormones. I found all this very interesting, but deeply troubling. Since nature was apparently not nearly as linear as our social constructs, how could I possibly determine what a Real Woman or a Real Man was? And if genetics was not the answer, where did that leave me?

Nevertheless I kept reading, because lots more studies were being published. It was discovered that a male seahorse gestates the eggs the female lays in his pouch. And the tropical clownfish changes its sex according to the reproductive needs of its community: if there are too many males, some of the fish simply transform into females (and vice-versa). But the one really contentious area of scientific study was with primates, because of all mammals, their DNA is the most similar to that of humans. Most researchers (typically male) were zealously measuring the testosterone levels in male primates, correlating increases in testosterone with heightened aggression. But these researchers were heartily debated by other researchers (typically female) who, by asking sophisticated questions, showed that in many cases it's the aggression that increases testosterone levels. At the height of this testosterone-correlates-with-aggression debate, it was found that macho activities such as war actually lower testosterone levels.

Dizzy, I put down the medical journals. But my much-needed intermission didn't last long. As more female scientists became prominent in their fields, they presented even more challenging data. A male orangutan becomes king of the roost only after first securing the affection and approval of the head female. Other female primates, such as monkeys and apes and especially bonobos, are sexually assertive and promiscuous with many partners, even when infertile or already pregnant. Until then, sexual activity for pleasure, rather than reproduction, was unheard of in animals.

And with hyenas, the females are much more aggressive than the males. There turned out to be lots of "exceptions" like these.

The irony of all these animal studies was that there was no guarantee they would apply to human biology or behavior. Just the same, I bought three more file cabinets to hold all the newspaper and journal articles I'd been stockpiling. By this time, even the local newspapers were featuring stories about the hormonal cycles of men as well as women, who now wouldn't have to take all the bad press for being emotional during their "time of the month." When I read that male monorail operators in Japan were prohibited from driving during the sensitive times of their cycles (never mind that these were biorhythm cycles), I couldn't help feeling smug.

I finally graduated college. But what should have been a celebration felt more like a funeral. I was no further along in my All-Encompassing Quest for Real Manhood and Real Womanhood than when I had begun my education. Although I was still clipping articles, I wasn't being paid to do all that reading, no matter how interesting it might be. So after several unsuccessful attempts at securing a conventional job, I found work singing and playing music for audiences in hospitals, nursing homes, and other institutional settings.

Meanwhile, the universe continued unraveling its secrets. As women in the business world (who got the jobs no one would hire me for) were battling corporate giants for paid maternity leave, scientists ascertained that the maternal instinct is hormonally stimulated by the mother's smelling of the newborn. I struggled with the possibility that maybe there was something to biology after all. But not too much, I hoped—that would only give men another excuse to call women weak and emotional, and order them back into the kitchen.

Frustrated, I did what came naturally to me: I collected more data, grateful for my "male" analytical mind and hating myself for even thinking in those terms. Maybe underneath my passion for learning was an inferior female body. But no! That couldn't be. Although females had less brute muscular strength than males, as a group they were found to be physically sturdier, more emotionally resilient, and often more impervious to disease. Didn't that count for something? Besides, the discovery had just been made that some men can lactate.

Trying to calm my whirling brain, I treated myself to New York City's Big Apple Circus and saw the first (and at that time, only) two-woman trapeze act in the world. I came away awed and gratified. One of the women had to be as strong as a man so she could hold not only herself in the air, but her partner too.

One day of socially redeeming entertainment, however, could not remedy years of alienation. All that time and effort devoted to my college education hadn't gotten me anywhere in my search for the Real Man or Real Woman. Although omnipresent—they were cultural fixtures, like bravery in war or the sanctity of motherhood—these Real individuals were nowhere to be found. I was exhausting my resources and running out of ideas. Where might I have overlooked them? Why couldn't I find them? What was I doing wrong?

Evidently, neither clothing nor behavior had anything to do with being a Real Man or a Real Woman. Neither did external genitalia, hidden genitalia, chromosomes, the sex of the person one relates to, sensitive times of the month, hormones, lactation ability, job earning power, or what someone does in their spare time. Moreover, one's gender role, biological sex, and sexual orientation were very different and distinct from each other. Neither literature, psychology, biology, nor genetics had clarified my search.

I felt defeated. Would I never know what it meant to be a Real Woman? And would I never know how to identify a Real Man? There had to be something definitive that would finally end my All-Encompassing Quest.

It's hard to say when the epiphany came. It might have been the night I was lying on the couch, eyes closed, listening to music because there was nothing left to read. Or maybe it came the morning I walked along the seashore, or the afternoon I went hiking in the woods. Perhaps the insight had always been there but was cloaked, the way the light seems to evaporate when clouds densely cover the sun. Eventually, I did hear the Voice. What began as a whisper became louder, more distinct, compelling. What exactly was I hearing?

It was my own inner knowing—this very wise, seasoned, confident Voice. It—I—had the answers all along, but could not recognize them as long as I gave more value to my parents' pestering, my classmates' teasing, thousands of pages turned, stacks of articles clipped and filed, too many boring discussion groups, endless rhetoric. Don't be too hard on yourself, I heard, every cell in my body vibrating like a bell. How can we know who we are until we sort through everything that isn't important, isn't us—isn't Real?

Since I began listening to my own Voice in earnest, I have learned a lot. I understand that we are all united by our humanity and our love. We wonder, cry, feel pissed and pleased, fight and forgive. Embracing the life force inside of myself that connects me to others is what makes me Real. I am no longer interested in classifying those whose chromosomes, hormones, genitalia, or species membership are different from my own. If I act on my desires responsibly, with respect and reverence toward myself and others, I don't need to justify myself with labels. When I'm in the present, being present, labels don't cross my mind. I'm too busy simply . . . being.

Decades after my mother's disparaging remarks, the sting has disappeared. I still walk like a soldier. But what was once a slur now represents strength. Yesterday's terrorization has become today's tribute. They call it "power walking."

Keila Matos

You Will Not Bully Me Anymore

I was hurt in the past, but of that there is no more
Yo pensé que el dolor destruiría mi honor; Pero yo me levanté la cara
    y dije:
You won't destroy me, no, no . . . you will not bully me anymore
I will keep on with my life
Y venceré este miedo
I will be stronger than what I am; you will not conquer my strength
Una vez más te diré
I will be strong
Venceré
Ganaré
I will bring light to my life
Seguiré adelante y triunfaré
With much effort I will learn y tendre una gran vida
You won't destroy me no, no . . . you will not bully me anymore
Why do you hurt me, I ask why? Why do you do this to us?
En el frio y el invierno encontrarás la verdad . . . No lastimes
No respires. Open your eyes and look for help!
Encontrarás la realidad, Una vez más te diré
I will be strong . . . Don't bully me anymore.

Emmy Cepeda
En el día de liberación

Tú un motivo de odio
Yo motivos de felicidad
Tú, otro de desprecio
Yo, el porque luchar.

Tú, un dolor desángrate
Yo, una luz que sana.
Tú, yo, un paso, adelante, atrás
Camino corto, camino largo.

Nos une la sangre, pero nos separa la libertad
Te molesta que puedo volar,
Y tú ni siquiera sabes como caminar
Luchas con la muerte, lucho con lo vivo.

Tú sigues tapando la verdad con un antifaz
Yo tapo el antifaz con la verdad
Tus cadenas ya no me pueden atar
Mi poder puede mucho más.

Ya deja de temerle a mí luz
Yo teme a tu oscuridad
Sal de esa cárcel y
Únete a luchar.

Emmy Cepeda

On the Day of Freedom
(translated by María Luisa Arroyo)

You, a reason to hate
I, reasons for joy
You, another who disdains and
I, the desire to fight.

You, a hemorrhagic sorrow
I, a light that heals.
You, I, a step, one forward, back
A short distance, a long walk.

Blood unifies us, but freedom separates us
It bothers you that I can fly
And you don't even know how to walk
You fight with death and I fight with what I live.

You keep covering the truth with a mask I cover the mask with truth
Your chains can no longer restrain me
My power is so much more.

Stop fearing now my light
And fear your own darkness
Leave that prison and
Join the fight.

Eilianie M. Alvelo

Mi intimo ser y mi ser

Cuando tus ojos pintados con burla, se aferran a mi mirada,
Cuando tus movimientos secos, bruscos deshidratan sus almas,
Cuando quieres que tus pasos lleguen al infierno en una sola zancada,
Cuando rujes y los leónes se acobijan en las palmas . . .

Pretendes que mis pestañas se apaguen,
Que mi alma dócil vaya al compás de mis pies tambaleantes,
Cuando sigilosamente;
Rozan las huellas de tu viento manipulante que gira en espiral.

¡Ay, so canto de . . . tú!
Hiciste un nudo en mis cuerdas vocales
Por mucho tiempo mi intimo ser no pudo respirar
Pero hoy la esperanza me escribe: "me voy a levantar,
Escucha el susurro y tú saldrás de estos caudales."

Y esa dulce voz me dice que aprenderé a sonreír,
Que si me enamoro de mi no temeré al rechazo,
Que honestamente sentiré el calor de un abrazo
Que con tanto anhelo mi íntimo ser quiere construir.

Mi intimo ser me busca y me quiere abrigar,
Me regala la fortaleza que llevo dentro.
Hoy tú no aterras mi alma y disfruto el encuentro.

Pues tus garras, no enganchan, ya no saben tambalear.

Mi intimo ser y mi ser, se persiguen y se abrazan.

Eilianie M. Alvelo

My Intimate Self and My Self
(translated by María Luisa Arroyo)

When your painted eyes mock and fix my gaze
When your dry and brusque movements dehydrate souls,
When you want your steps to reach hell in one leap
When you flood and the lions unearth themselves in the palm trees . . .

Pretend that my eyelashes are extinguished,
That my docile soul will go to the beat of my unsteady feet
When silently
The imprints of your manipulative breath journeying in spirals.

Oh you piece of . . . you!
You knotted my vocal cords
For so long my intimate self could not breathe
But today hope is writing to me: "I am going to rise,
Listen to the whisper and you will emerge from that flow."

And that sweet voice tells me that I will learn how to smile,
That if I fall in love with myself I will not fear rejection,
That honestly I will feel the warmth of an embrace
That with such longing my intimate self desires to make.

My intimate self looks for me and wants to shelter me,
It grants me the strength that I carry within.
Today, you don't terrorize my soul and I enjoy the encounter
For your claws don't grab, now that they no longer know how to move.

My intimate self and my self pursue each other and embrace.

María Luisa Arroyo

One Mother's Response to Sirdeaner's Call

for Sirdeaner Walker

A few weeks before Carl's death,
you and I ran into each other at the Y
and stood at the edge of the track
with your patient daughter
as we talked about single motherhood
and private schools and did what mothers do:
exude joy about all our children.

Upstairs, in the Family Zone, our sons,
polite strangers, huffed and grunted
and clocked time on the tread mill,
on the weight bench, on the air hockey table,
and on the ever-popular Wii games.
In the shuffle of sign-outs and backpacks,
all of our lives touched briefly.

Full-time co-workers by day,
we returned to our weeknight routines
of driving home to wash up, cook dinner,
help with homework, wash the dishes, play
a board game or watch some TV, coax our kids
to their rooms at nine, and, finally, we collapsed
on a couch that, more often than not, becomes our bed.

A few weeks later, Carl hanged himself.

Even as a mother, I cannot imagine the discovery
that sucked you suddenly
through the plate glass window of grief.
Millions of shards of invisible glass

embedded themselves in all of your organs,
—not just in your heart. They still erupt
through your soulskin. Sadness, you said,
has now become your companion.

A few days later, you spoke out in the newspaper.

And that is when you began to feel the pain
as administrators and teachers at your son's school,
and key members of our community, acted
just like the very bystanders who watched your child
be bullied for months: they said and did nothing.
The silence of so many wrapped like a shroud
around you and you felt the shards press back in.

And still, you speak out in Carl's memory,
whose presence you still feel daily
as you pack school lunches, glance in the rearview
mirror to count heads, rush from schools to work,
touch the football jersey that hung so loosely
on his hopeful body, set the dinner table, send
each child to bed before the couch claims you.

Faith, one of your life rafts, is a dove that flies
through a stained-glass window and survives.

Your mission now is to speak out, even to those
who refuse to listen, about how bullying matters,
how those who cry out are not only the targeted
but also the bullies, how students, teachers, and parents
need to step forward and not step back, how parents
should be able to take for granted that their children—
regardless of their ages—should feel safe
as they are being educated.

Sirdeaner Walker, I add my voice to yours.
My students, with their letters, add their voices to yours.

Magdalena Gómez and Teatro V!da add their voices to yours.
Springfield community members, add your voices to ours.

As the new school year begins, let our voices and our words
reverberate through school halls and interrupt the routine of silence.
Let us interrupt the dismissive wave of a teacher's hand,
the dismissive look in a counselor's face,
the whispers and the knowing glances of students
whenever a child or a teen dares to share
that she is being bullied or that he is being taunted.

Let all teachers, administrators, and parents remember
a time in their lives when they were bullied or were bullies,
or a time in their lives when they stood by and did nothing,
yes, let's make them understand that,
despite how often it occurs,
to bully or to be bullied
is not a rite of passage.

Sam Plotkin
(written at age thirteen)

Make It Through

Have you ever wanted to show the world what really matters?
Have you ever noticed that life doesn't come on a silver platter?
But it still comes—in any shape or form.
And when no one cares, what matters to you doesn't matter to them
You feel torn in two.

But you can make it through
With all the things that you do
You can show the world you
So you can make it through
and be the one that people never knew
And however life comes to you
You can make it through

Do you see your future in your dreams and watch where you go?
Do you wish someday you could be in those dreams that you sow?
And be free from all the controversy
And fly away to the place where you belong
And feel brand new

Oh you can make it through
With all the things that you do
You can show the world you
So you can make it through
and be the one that people never knew
And however life comes to you
You can make it through

Life comes at you fast
But life doesn't control you
Though people will step on you
Or walk around you

In life it's okay to feel
We better make it through in our own way
Before the world goes insane

Oh you can make it through
With all the things that you do
You can show the world you
you can make it through
and be the one that people never knew
And however life comes to you
You'll still make it through

Eilish Thompson

A Bully Pesticide

No. What I used to be was a reaction so subliminal
to your unconditional bondage of ignorance
additional to your behavior so criminal.
I used to be just a stray red mark in your book,
condemned "unfit" for society's brand-name look
because of appearance—
a straight shot to a truly tormented soul,
and in the control of the steady flow
of self esteem to the heart, an interference.

And so I used to feel that I must saturate myself inside these lines
inside the confines of your wordy fists,
and felt by those in authority to be just another
punctuation mark in your transitional times, 20 or rather hit lists.

My trampled feelings were a miniscule complication
in a daily journalized compilation of all the hurtful situations
you found in your appalling soul the right to be the catalyst to.
Completely forgotten by the underhanded will of still logic,
and by the system, played and misused.

You used to plague my thoughts with an undeserved of amount of stress,
and would beat your chest to show your "boldness"—as if it were a test,
but when the administrators pointed fingers, you would protest.

You were allowed to sneer with nostrils running gossip
and create scars which would be reminders of your days.
But I have conquered and have fought through
your gripping, malevolent ways.

And while you were connecting the dots of your pitiful life,
I was counting the syllables it would take to give you
a grammatically correct piece of personal strife—

Magdalena Gómez and *María Luisa Arroyo* 243

honestly inspired by the different versions of your taunts
which now fail to give me even haunts.

Because after years of attempting to get this message through to no avail,
I've learned that it is we who must not let evil prevail,
though the world promises the best for those who transgress,
and it is we who must be firm in attaining the peaceful right
for all—else we shall see the civilization we claim to have continue to fall.
There may continue to be people like you
who sneer and honestly think they are the best—
the cream of the crop, the ones on the top—
but in reality are clichés like all the rest.

So beyond what I know and who I know I've become
far past the potholes I used to sit in sucking my thumb,
beyond the doleful confines of the school yard,
I learned that true, real living isn't even close to as hard.

Because I've found my niche,
a way of communicating through what I always held back—
something you can't hold under attack—
for you can't offend these lines, carefully crafted in their designs.

I've acquired a pair of newer, bigger, brighter and fuller eyes
and I see what the future holds—and it lacks your lies
about how my looks aren't what they should be.
A bully is all you'll ever prove to be—
and now you have become a miniscule stain on my sleeve, permanently.

Contributors' Notes

Janet E. Aalfs, a 2003–2005 Poet Laureate of Northampton, MA, has directed since 1982 Valley Women's Martial Arts: Institute for Healing and Violence-Prevention Strategies, a non-profit school in Easthampton. Aalfs has taught and performed weavings of poetry and martial arts dance at many venues including the 2008 Dodge Poetry Festival in New Jersey; an international exchange project in Cape Town, South Africa; St. Marks Place in New York City; and "Split This Rock" Poetry Festival in Washington, DC. *Bird of a Thousand Eyes* (Levellers Press, 2010) is Aalfs' most recent full-length book of poems and her writing has been published in numerous journals and anthologies.

Judge William (Hank) Abrashkin, a native of New York City and graduate of Columbia University and Western New England College School of Law, had a law practice on Cape Cod and in Boston. Abrashkin was then appointed by Governor Dukakis as First Justice of the Massachusetts Housing Court, Western Massachusetts Division, a position he served for 22 years. In 2008, he left the judiciary to assume his current position as Executive Director of the Springfield Housing Authority (MA). A central focus of Judge Abrashkin's work as lawyer, judge, and housing authority director has been to work with at-risk families and children as they struggle with the obstacles and disadvantages of their circumstances.

Li Yun Alvarado is a poet, writer, and educator whose work has been published in several journals including *The Acentos Review, Kweli Journal, PMS poemmemoirstory, PALABRA,* and *Modern Haiku.* She is currently a doctoral candidate in English at Fordham University where she helps to coordinate Fordham's Poets Out Loud reading series. She lives in New York City and takes frequent trips to Salinas, Puerto Rico to visit la familia.

Eilianie M. Alvelo es una joven poeta cuya cuna yace en Comerío, Puerto Rico desde el 1992. A temprana edad mostró su genuíno interés por las artes y los deportes. A los 12 años de edad se alejó de su hogar para ir a la escuela olímpica especializada en deportes E.C.E.D.A.O. en Salinas, Puerto Rico. Después de tres años en E.C.E.D.A.O. tuvo que mudarse a Springfield, Massachusetts debido a las delicadas condiciones de salud de su madre. Hoy día, solo el arte y su continua búsqueda por educación la acompañan. Es parte de un grupo teatral llamado "Teatro V!da" y estudia psicología en Bay Path College. www.eilianie.weebly.com

Michael Amato, currently a freshman at Holyoke Community College (Holyoke, MA), resides in West Springfield, MA with his parents, brother, and cat. A 2009 graduate of West Springfield High School, the torments he faced there are still fresh, breathing in the asbestos in the hallways and seeing the face of the boy that pummeled him to the ground. His verbal handicap, apraxia, has been a contributor to the pain. While life is a struggle, Amato aspires to open his own store retailing in skateboard merchandise.

Diego Angarita-Horowitz, the Food Systems Organizer for Nuestras Raíces (Holyoke, MA), is in charge of coordinating the food policy change component of the Community Action Plan for the Holyoke Food and Fitness Policy Council. As an organizer he coordinates the youth program, works with community food producers off season and sits on the Massachusetts Food Policy Alliance. A 2008 graduate of Hampshire College in 2008, Angarita-Horowitz focused on the intersections of colonization, media studies, and nutrition.

María Luisa Arroyo, editor, is a Massachusetts Cultural Council grant recipient in poetry and author of *Gathering Words: Recogiendo Palabras* (Bilingual Press: 2008) and the self-published chapbook, *Touching and Naming the Roots of This Tree* (2009), is a Puerto Rican poet, educator, a well-traveled polyglot, teaching artist and passionate advocate of family literacy and the arts. Educated at Colby, Tufts, and Harvard, Arroyo has facilitated numerous poetry workshops regionally including at Mount Holyoke College and performed nationally, including in the PALABRA PURA Series in Chicago, IL and in Puerto Rico. Many of Arroyo's individual poems have been published in journals such as *PALABRA, CALYX,* and *The Women's Review of Books*. www.marialuisaarroyo.weebly.com

Janis Astor del Valle, a Puerto Rican lesbian, writer, performer and filmmaker, holds an MFA in Film from Columbia University and a BA in Theatre from Marymount Manhattan College. Janis is currently touring her two solo plays: *Trans Plantations*, which explores her identity crisis as a Nuyorican lesbian uprooted from her Bronx barrio and transplanted to rural Connecticut; and, *Becoming Joaquin*, about a transgendered Latino's struggle for acceptance. She resides in New Haven, CT, with her wife. www.janisastor.com

Albert Bermel, PhD, has taught theatre, including Shakespeare's comedies, at Columbia University, Yale School of Drama, the Julliard School, the Graduate Center of CUNY and Lehman College. He is the author of numerous plays and books, including *The Infernal Machine and Other Plays*, and the seminal *Artaud's Theater of Cruelty*. He is also a translator and written about two hundred essays and theatre reviews for *The New Leader*.

Emmy Cepeda, a seventeen-year-old actress and writer born and raised in Santiago, Dominican Republic, is currently a student at Springfield Technical Community College(STCC), in Springfield, MA and an ensemble member of Teatro V!da. Emmy plans to become a cardiologist. www.emmycepeda.weebly.com

Susan Cleveland, a Springfield (MA) native, moved from one part of the city to another, until she went away to college. After graduating, she spent most of her career working in a variety of mental health jobs, as well as, writing and doing music on the side. She currently lives in Greenfield (MA) with two rescued cats that often find their way into her stories.

Robin Coolbeth grew up in Springfield (MA) in a family with a love for books and the arts. For many years, she has been a participant in the Springfield Central Library's Open Mic Poetry Series organized by Crystal Senter Brown and in poetry workshops facilitated by María Luisa Arroyo. She works at UMASS Amherst and participated in a series of writing workshops for employees, which was offered by the Labor/Management Workplace Education Program.

Ronald Coolbeth, born in 1932 in Lyndonville, VT, has always been interested in writing and art, more specifically, painting. Some of his poems and short stories have been published and his story on bullying is true.

Lori Desrosiers' full-length poetry collection, *The Philosopher's Daughter*, is being published by Salmon Poetry at the end of 2012. Desrosiers' chapbook, *Three Vanities* (Pudding House Press: 2009) chronicles three generations of women in her family. In 2010, her poem "That Pomegranate Shine" won the Greater Brockton Society for Poetry and the Arts Award for New England Poets. She is the publisher and managing editor of *Naugatuck River Review*, a journal of narrative poetry.

Mary E. Delabruere is the mother of one adult daughter, Shannon. A Western Massachusetts resident who works as a registered nurse, Delabruere has been writing poetry since childhood.

Carolyn Durán, a seventeen-year-old writer and performance poet born and raised in Santo Domingo, Dominican Republic, is currently a student at Springfield Technical Community College (STCC), an ensemble member of Teatro V!da and an active member of Desprendimiento en Acción.

Ameer Kim El-Mallawany is a Korean Egyptian nomad from the steel and suburban sprawl of the Midwest. After a decade out East, he has returned home to continue his journey as a schoolteacher, often inspired by the words of our young poets, writers, and storytellers.

Sandra María Esteves' poetry collections include *Bluestown Mockingbird Mambo* (Arte Público Press:1990), and her first book of poetry, *Yerba Buena* (Greenfield Review Press: 1980) was selected as the "Best Small Press" by the Library Journal. Her awards include a Pregones Theater/NEA Master Artist Award, the Con Tinta Award from Acentos/AWP, and a Poetry Fellowship from NYFA. A teaching artist for over thirty years, she has conducted workshops for the NYC Board of Education, Teachers & Writers Collaborative, the Bronx Council on the Arts and the Caribbean Cultural Center. A believer that creativity is the antithesis to violence, Esteves has presented her work at major educational and cultural institutions across the country. Esteves' writings focus on transformation and empowerment through reflection and analysis of real life issues. For more info go to www. SandraEsteves.com.

Jennifer Anne Fasulo (1967–2010), dedicated her life to a passionate struggle of advocating for human rights, social and economic justice for all oppressed peoples. Jennifer applied her gifts in filmmaking, teaching, adult basic education, counseling, radio production, writing and poetry, to the benefit of humanity. She was a housing advocate, fought for and helped create free day-care at the University of Massachusetts, Amherst; helped to create an Affirmative Action Fund at the University; spearheaded the activist group, SOWFI, Solidarity of Women's Freedom in Iraq; was a women's and LGBTQ activist and she co-wrote, directed and produced the film, *Primetime: Fighting Back Against Foreclosure,* which premiered at the Museum of Modern Art in New York City, and was her final film project. Her life and legacy continue to bear fruit in the countless lives she touched and transformed.

Nakeishy Marie Fontán Sanchez, a middle school student in a Holyoke Public School, is actively involved in Girls Inc. of Holyoke and likes to write poetry.

Gabriel Fontes was born September 1, 1996, in Greenfield, Massachusetts. Raised by a Portuguese father and a Jewish mother, Gabriel developed an early interest in world cultures. His excerpt takes place in Buenos Aires, Argentina.

Lisa Aronson Fontes, PhD, is on the faculty of University without Walls at the University of Massachusetts, Amherst, where she helps adults complete their college degrees and realize their dreams. She has dedicated two decades to making the mental health, social service, and criminal justice systems more responsive to culturally diverse people. Fontes is the author of books and articles on cultural issues regarding child maltreatment and violence against women. And she's not a bully, really.

Magdalena Gómez, editor, is the recipient of numerous grants and awards, and was designated a Master Artist by National Endowment for the Arts presenters, Pregones Theater, NYC. She is a multi-disciplinary artist, columnist, educator and national keynote speaker. Magdalena is also a commentator with National Public Radio. Publishing credits include: *The Progressive*; *The Berkshire Review*; *Ollantay Theater Journal*;

Palabra: A Magazine of Chicano and Latino Literary Art; *Houghton Mifflin*; and the *L.A. Times*. Venues include: The Brooklyn Academy of Music; Vanderbilt University and the Department of Social and Health Services in Washington. Her plays for children and adults have been presented nationally, including Off-broadway and in countless schools. She has been a teaching artist throughout the United States and abroad since 1974. www.latinapoet.net; www.teatrovida.com; www.bestkeynotes.com

José B. Gonzalez is the co-editor of *Latino Boom: An Anthology of U.S. Latino Literature* and LatinoStories.com. He has published poetry in various anthologies and journals including *Callaloo*, *PALABRA,* and the *Quercus Review*, and he has been a contributor to National Public Radio. An award-winning educator and poet and resident of Quaker Hill, CT, Gonzalez has been a featured speaker at colleges and universities throughout the country.

Arjuna Greist is a writer, musician, radio DJ, and performance poet from Northampton, MA. A believer that the pen is truly mightier than the sword, Arjuna wields words in an ongoing battle for peace and justice. Audio of "bad little soldier" and other songs, along with tour and album info, can be found at www.arjunagreist.com.

Shel Horowitz's Apex Award-winning eighth book, *Guerrilla Marketing Goes Green*, which you can preview at greenandprofitable.com, covers the Save the Mountain story in much more detail. It also shows business owners how to succeed with ethics and social/environmental justice. A resident of Hadley, MA, Horowitz writes the internationally syndicated "Green and Profitable" column.

Susan Hucul, a Springfield (MA) native, an experienced ELL and reading teacher in the Springfield Public Schools and active presenter at schools and professional development workshops on ELL and reading, works as a district literacy coach to eight schools in Springfield. In this position, Hucul assists principals, instructional leaders and teachers in implementing best literacy practices for all children. Hucul holds a degree in ELL and Reading from the University of Massachusetts, Amherst and has completed additional Master's level work in Special Education from Cambridge College.

Angela Kariotis is creator of the solo shows "Reminiscence of the Ghetto & Other Things that Raized Me, "Say Logos Say Word," and "Stretch Marks." Kariotis' awards include the National Performance Network Creation Fund Award, New Jersey State Council on Arts Playwriting Fellowship, and Tennessee Williams Theater Fellowship. Among her presenters are University of California-Los Angeles, Hip Hop Theater Festival in New York City, Legion Arts in Iowa, and Contact Theater in United Kingdom. For artist info and video visit: www.angelakaRIOTis.com.

Rick Kearns, a poet, freelance writer and percussionist with Flamenco Aquí y Ahora based in Harrisburg, PA, has had poems published in many journals, including the *Massachusetts Review*, the *Painted Bride Quarterly*, and *Chicago Review*. Kearns' work has been featured in four national anthologies and he has performed his poetry throughout the US since 1992. Some of his work has been translated into Spanish and Portuguese and has been read aloud on radio shows in Argentina and Brazil. In addition, Kearns is a Latin America correspondent for Indian Country Today and many of his articles have been reprinted, one in a Native American Studies text.

Linda Keiderling was born in Springfield, MA, and at the age of ten, when her family moved to Chicopee, MA, she met her first two bullies. Keiderling loves to read and write poetry and short stories. This is her second publication.

John Kuebler is a 2009 NEA Arts Journalism fellow and the 2008 Buffalo National River Writer in Residence. Kuebler's plays have been produced by the Actors Theatre of Louisville and Axial Theatre Company and read by Su Teatro and the Rocky Mountain Theatre Association. He lives in Denver with his son.

Priscilla LaBoy was working toward her GED at MCDI in Springfield, MA, at the time that this poem was written.

Diane Lefer is a playwright and author whose works for the stage include *Nightwind*, created in collaboration with Colombian exile and torture survivor Hector Aristizábal, which has toured the US, Canada, and the world (including Colombia and Afghanistan) for the anti-torture movement. They are also co-authors of the nonfiction book, *The Blessing Next to the Wound: A Story of Art, Activism, and Transformation* (Lantern Books: 2010). Her most recent book-length fiction, *California Transit* (Sarabande Books: 2007), received the Mary McCarthy Prize. Lefer has offered writing and theatre workshops for California youth both in and coming out of the juvenile in/justice system.

Janice Levy is the author of numerous children's books, among them *Alley Oops!,* a picture book about bullying, told from the bully's perspective, and about hurt and anger, empathy and hope, resilience and ingenuity. It's about that "alley oops!" moment when a child experiences empowerment and self-esteem that come from doing the right thing. For more information, go to www.janicelevy.com.

Sara Littlecrow-Russell has been published in a wide variety of magazines, journals, and anthologies including: *The Massachusetts Review, American Indian Quarterly, Race Traitor, Flyaway, Red Ink, Yellow Medicine Review, U.S. Latino Review, Sister Nations: Native American Women Writing on Community; Yellow as Tumeric, Fragrant as Cloves: An Asian Women's Anthology;* the erotic anthology *Touched by Eros,* and *Pro Libertad.* Her first book of poetry, *The Secret Power of Naming,* was named Outstanding Book of 2007 by the Gustavus Myers Center for the Study of Bigotry and Human Rights and received a bronze medal from the Independent Publisher's Association.

Ruth Margraff's writings have been presented nationally and internationally. Margraff's work is published by *Dramatists Play Service, Kendall/Hunt, Backstage Books, DramaReview, Performing Arts Journal, American Theatre, Theater Forum, Playscripts, Inc.* and many others. Margraff has taught playwriting at the Yale School of Drama, Brown University, University of Texas/Michener Center for Writers and is Associate Professor at the School of the Art Institute of Chicago. www.RuthMargraff.com

Iris Morales, born and raised in New York City, is an activist, educator, filmmaker, television producer, and labor attorney. Morales' work has been shaped and inspired by the Puerto Rican people's dynamic struggles for justice and vibrant contributions in music, arts, and politics and has fought for

the rights of Latinos/Latinas, African Americans, and other working people. Morales is also the co-founder of two organizations to educate young
people in media literacy and video production. www.us-puertoricans.org

Keila Matos is an ensemble member of Teatro V!da. She was a writer
and performer in Teatro V!da's original production of *Bullying: What
Are You Going to Do About It?* and the upcoming touring production of
WH?TCHULOOK!NAT?

LaDonna J. Olanyk, a 1980 college graduate of Elementary Education, has
worked with children in grades preschool through fourth grade, including
those with Special Needs and those from low-income families. Throughout her teaching career, Olanyk has witnessed many children being tormented by bullies. Much of her poetry deals with the adversity and distress
that many children deal with on a daily basis.

Nina Lydia Olff, M.Ed, is a poet, visual artist, former educator and re-
searcher. She grew up in the Brownsville section of Brooklyn NY during
the 1960's and comes from an African-American, Russian-Jewish, Suri-
namese and American Indian family. She believes that Art, Education and
Social Justice make a golden triangle.

Judith Ortiz Cofer was born in Puerto Rico and raised in Paterson, New
Jersey, Judith Ortiz Cofer now makes her home in Athens, Georgia. She
is a poet, essayist, and novelist, whose work explores the experience of
being Puerto Rican and living, writing, and teaching in the United States.
Ortiz Cofer is the author of numerous books in multiple genres. She is the
Regents' and Franklin Professor of English and Creative Writing at the
University of Georgia. Cofer was inducted into the Georgia Writers Hall of
Fame in 2009. Work reprinted with permission from the author.

Carlos David Palacio, a Teatro V!da ensemble member, attends Springfield High School of Science and Technology and plays baseball. His future
plans are to get an MBA and start his own business.

Suni Paz, an Argentine singer, songwriter, poet, educator, author, presenter and recipient of numerous awards, has devoted her life to children

and their families. She has thrilled worldwide audiences of all ages on stage, television and radio with her stories and songs accompanied on guitar, charango and percussive instruments. In 2007, Paz published her memoirs in Spanish *Destellos y Sombras* and in English, *Sparkles and Shadows*. For more information, go to www.sunipaz.com, and www.folkways.si.edu.

Vanessa Otero studied Women's Studies at Smith College and Public Policy at UMASS. Self-identified as a member of a growing network of mentors and mentees, Otero works to create forums and collaborations with the goal of highlighting the power within her community.

Tess Pfeifer, a recipient of the Massachusetts Cultural Council's Artist Grant in poetry, has written poetry all her life. This past year, Pfeifer was a judge for the Massachusetts Book Awards in Poetry and a readers' guide writer for the Massachusetts Center for the Book. A dedicated librarian for the Springfield Renaissance School, Pfeifer continues to write poetry for children and adults, as well as review books and serve on poetry committees. Her poems for children can be found at http://writtenforchildren. blogspot.com.

Evan Plotkin is the President and Managing Director of NAI Plotkin, a Springfield-based real estate firm that is recognized as a leader in commercial brokerage companies representing the industrial, retail, and medical/office markets. At present, the firm manages over 6 million sq. ft. of residential, industrial, retail, and medical/office buildings, of which approximately 1 million sq. ft. is located in Springfield. Plotkin has many other interests and currently serves on the Board of Forest Park Zoological Society, the Somers Education Foundation, the Center for Human Development, the Springfield Library and Museum Association, City Stage and Symphony Hall, and the Springfield Business Improvement District, among others.

Sam Plotkin is a singer-songwriter and performer from Somers, Connecticut who lives in Nashville, where he has recently recorded two CD's of original music with producer and friend Cliff Downs. Sam has been a featured soloist since the age of eight with a steadily growing fan base, and has performed in many venues including the MassMutual Center,

Six Flags New England, Springfield Symphony Hall, the Iron Horse Music Hall, Theodore's, the Majestic Theater, and the Big E—Eastern States Exposition. After early acceptances to Berklee College of Music in Boston and Belmont University in Nashville, he has chosen to attend Belmont where he was admitted as a Songwriting major to the Curb College of Entertainment and Music Business. www.samplotkin.com

Puma Perl's poetry and fiction have been published in over 100 print and online journals and anthologies. Her first chapbook, *Belinda and Her Friends* (2008) was awarded the Erbacce Press 2009 Poetry Award, and a full-length collection, *knuckle tattoos*, was published in early 2010. Perl performs her work in many venues, in and out of New York City. She is the co-founder of DDAY Productions, and curates a monthly event at the Yippie Museum Café. For more information, check out http://pumaperl.blogspot.com.

Mirtha Quiroz, born in Puerto Plata, Dominican Republic, was raised in Santo Domingo and later in Santurce, Puerto Rico. She holds a Bachelor's degree in Art from Westfield State College and a Masters degree in Spanish Literature from Middlebury College. Quiroz is a painter who expresses a wide range of women's experiences through her work and her Caribbean heritage is evident in her expressions of everyday life through her paintings.

Jha'nai Richardson, born in New Haven, CT, was a sixteen-year-old junior at South Gwinnett High School in Snellville, Georgia, at the time that her piece was accepted to this anthology. Richardson enjoys reading, writing, and acting, is an active member of the Thespian Society, and plans to pursue a career as a crime scene investigator.

Alvaro Saar Rios, a playwright and performer, is a former student of Pulitzer Prize winning playwrights Edward Albee and Lanford Wilson and is the founder of the national performance troupe The Royal Mexican Players. An MFA graduate from Northwestern University, Saar Rios lives and teaches theatre in Milwaukee (WI). For more information, visit: www.royalmexicans.com.

Edwin Rodríguez is currently a student at Dean Tech (Holyoke, MA) and is engaged in the Computer Technology and Data Communication workshop. At the time that this poem was written, Rodríguez was a student at the Peck School (Holyoke, MA). Rodríguez likes to write short stories and poems.

Yolanda Maria-Rose Scavron, a graduate of Holyoke Community College, is currently attending Saint Peter's College in New Jersey. Scavron has always had a strong belief in the arts as an advocate for change, and has enjoyed her time working with Teatro V!da in support of that cause. Scavron hopes to graduate soon with a degree in Urban Studies and will be able to continue to work with programs such as this. Scavron is a founding youth member of Teatro V!da, and currently an alumna and artistic associate.

Cathy J. Schlund-Vials is an Assistant Professor in English and Asian American Studies at the University of Connecticut at Storrs. She is also the Associate Director of the UConn Asian American Studies Institute. Her research interests include refugee cultural production, critical race theory, and contemporary ethnic American literary studies. Schlund-Vials' work has appeared in *Life Writing, Embodying Asian/American Sexualities* (edited by Sean Metzger and Gina Masquesmay), and *Journal of Asian American Studies*. She is the author of *Modeling Citizenship: Naturalization in Jewish and Asian American Writing* (Temple University Press: 2011), and is currently working on her second book, which is focused on Cambodian American genocide remembrance (forthcoming, University of Minnesota Press).

Nenah Sylver received her PhD in psychology and holistic health in 1996 from The Union Institute. Despite her mother's exclamation, "Don't you stick with anything?" Nenah has enjoyed all of her many careers: as a singer/songwriter, body-mind (Reichian) psychotherapist, holistic health educator, and author. Sylver's writing on feminism, sexuality, the natural sciences and complementary health has appeared in *Townsend Letter, Nexus, Natural Food & Farming*, and the anthologies *Closer to Home: Bisexuality and Feminism* (Seal Press), *Transforming A Rape Culture* (Milkweed Editions), and *Women, Culture, and Society: Readings in Women's Studies* (Simon and Schuster). www.nenahsylver.com

Teatro V!da, the first Springfield, MA, based Latino theater, was the vision of Magdalena Gómez. In 2007, the Latino Breakfast Club helped her to acquire start-up funds and gather community support to launch the project. Youth ensemble members activate their creativity as building blocks for literacy, leadership and civic engagement through the arts. They write and perform new works for the stage, radio and video; learn to design and facilitate training workshops in theater, for peers and adults; and produce their own events. Ensemble members are working in collaboration with www.amherstmedia.org to study and apply civic journalism. Intergenerational collaborations with master artists have included: internationally acclaimed composers, bandleaders and musicians—Fred Ho; Taylor Ho Bynum; Abraham Gomez-Delgado; Rene Gonzalez; and Heshima Moja. Moja is also the Music Director of Teatro V!da. Other master artists include: media maker and human rights activist, Iris Morales; poet and visual artist, Sandra María Esteves; theater director, Daniel Jáquez; four-time Grammy winner, guitarist, Victor Rosario; Bomba dancer Lydia Pérez, and Poet in Residence, María Luisa Arroyo, among many others. www.teatrovida.com

Narelle Thomas, seventeen, is a visual and performing artist from Springfield MA. She thinks that we can prosper if we give of ourselves truly, and love ourselves and those around us. Thomas feels that if we stand for what we believe in, we can create our own change. A member of the Teatro V!da ensemble, Thomas seeks to help uplift and give to her community through positive action.

Eilish Thompson is the type of woman to first imagine through imagery; the type who can picture a better future through art, pun intended. She holds a firm belief in the infallible ability of the arts to unite communities, nations, ethnicities and egos. Thompson further believes that it is through the implementation of the arts as a constant and driving force in our everyday lives that humanity will (re-)realize what it is to act humanely and civility will be (re-)valued in civilization. Thompson is a proud Teatro V!da member, a 2010 Springfield Public School graduate and one of those people who is invested in the tangible change and freedom that the arts grant. www.souledtohope.weebly.com

Marian Tombri, the oldest of six siblings who grew up on the mean streets of the South End of Springfield, is a self-described young woman with enormous dreams who will achieve them through the use of words, her pen, and her passion for coffee and tea. At Westfield State, Tombri earned a Bachelor's in business management and marketing. Tombri's ultimate dream is to own a coffee and tea café while still painting and creating poetry. She dove headfirst into this thing called poetry and never looked back.

Sources

Janis Astor del Valle: "Trans Plantations," original version published in *Action: The Nuyorican Poets Cafe Theater Festival*, 1996. Reprinted with permission of the author.

Albert Bermel: "The Mountain Chorus" published in *The Mountain Chorus, Six One-Act Farces by Albert Bermel*, Oracle Press, 1982. Play reprinted with permission of the author.

Judith Ortiz Cofer: "The Welcome Mat," first published in "Lessons from A Writer's Life, Readings and Resources for Teachers and Students; Heinemann, Portsmouth, NH, 2011. Reprinted with permission of the author.

José B. Gonzalez: "i couldn't for a teenaged bully's death," first published in Acentos Review, 2008. Reprinted with permission of the author.

Arjuna Greist: "bad little soldier," self-published liner notes for album, *odd numbers,* copyright, 2003, apple fall records. Reprinted with permission of the author.

Suni Paz: "Alias, La Nata" self-published in Spanish: *Destellos y Sombras de la Inocencia a la Madurez*, February 2007. TXVI-070-088; in English, Sparkles and Shadows from Innocence to Wisdom, May 2007. Reprinted with permission of the author.

Alvaro Saar Rios: "Brown Enough," self-published in: A Trip Through the Mind of a "Crazy Mexican, chapbook, Houston, TX. Copyright 2006. Reprinted with permission of the author.